M000023168

THINK
AND GROW
THROUGH
ART AND
MUSIC

THINK
AND GROW
THROUGH
ART AND
MUSIC

FOR ANYONE ASPIRING TO BECOME A
PROFESSIONAL ARTIST AND / OR MUSICIAN

Over 20 Years of Interviews and Research
Beginning with Chet Atkins, Les Paul
and a Wide Catalogue of Artistry

RANDEY W. FAULKNER
WRITTEN IN COOPERATION WITH
THE NAPOLEON HILL FOUNDATION

MEDIA

Published 2020 by Gildan Media LLC
aka G&D Media
www.GandDmedia.com

Copyright © 2020 by The Napoleon Hill Foundation

No part of this book may be used, reproduced or transmitted in any manner whatsoever, by any means (electronic, photocopying, recording, or otherwise), without the prior written permission of the author, except in the case of brief quotations embodied in critical articles and reviews. No liability is assumed with respect to the use of the information contained within. Although every precaution has been taken, the author and publisher assume no liability for errors or omissions. Neither is any liability assumed for damages resulting from the use of the information contained herein.

Interior design by Meghan Day Healey of Story Horse, LLC.

Library of Congress Cataloging-in-Publication Data is available upon request

ISBN: 978-1-7225-0363-5

10   9   8   7   6   5   4   3   2   1

Contents

QR Code Instructions

Let me explain what QR Codes are, how to use them, and their purpose. At the end of each chapter you will find a QR code, which stands for "Quick Response." By scanning this code with your smart phone, it will perform one of two tasks; First, on the pages marked "Video," the QR code will unlock exclusive video narration by the master himself, Dr. Napoleon Hill. Consider it an honor to hear the Master's voice. Second, on the pages marked "Audio Only," the QR code will unlock spoken narration.

The QR codes recap key points relating to the exciting topic you have just read. With most smart phones, follow these simple instructions.

1. Tap your camera icon.
2. Hover the device steady for 2–3 seconds over the QR code you want to scan. You will know it has been read when a notification appears at the top of your screen.
3. Tap the naphill.org notification at the top of your screen.
4. Tap the arrow to open the content of the QR code.

Please note; Some phones might require you to download an App for a QR code scanner. Most are free. Once downloaded, follow the above steps 2–4.

Regarding the quality of the QR video codes; No doubt when you view these videos you will first notice their age, as they appear in black and white. Please excuse the minor glitches and try to get the most from what the Master is relaying.

It's the old saying, "When the student is ready, the teacher will appear." Enjoy with an open and Positive Mental Attitude!

Note: If you have any technical difficulties with the QR codes please contact the author at randeyfaulkner@gmail.com.

Note

Randey Faulkner has spent his life around musicians and artists. During a twenty year period, he gained a vast amount of knowledge from legendary icons, and I know you will enjoy reading about them in this book. Randey does an excellent job of helping you reach your goals using the success principles that Napoleon Hill spent his life studying.

All of the writings in this book just help to confirm the fact that action is required if you want to be successful. You must first develop a definite purpose, then you must put those plans into action to achieve that dream. By applying the principles you read in *Think and Grow Through Art and Music* and taking action in your own life, you will greatly enhance your chance of succeeding. After all, isn't that what you want?

Don Green
Executive Director
Napoleon Hill Foundation

Foreword

This story is taken from Billy Ray Cyrus's book, *Hillbilly Heart*, written in 2013. He shares how he was first introduced to Napoleon Hill and *Think and Grow Rich*. He testifies to the strength and validity of this science of success philosophy and how it has helped him succeed.

It was a beautiful spring day in 1980, as Billy Ray was driving to work. He noticed a nice car stopped on the side of the road. Standing next to it was an older gentleman with white hair, wearing a business suit. Billy Ray stopped and asked, "Sir are you ok?"

"Yes, I'm alright," the man said. "You know it's a unique quality today for a person of your age to stop and help a man in need, don't you think?"

Billy Ray said, "I just wanted to make sure you were ok."

The older gentleman then said, "I would like to ask you something son." He continued, "When you stopped here, you gave me something. You gave me your time. The fact that you cared whether I was ok, speaks volumes about your character, that's a rare quality son. I want to give you something in return. How would you like to know the secret that could lead you to see, have, or do anything you want in this world?"

Billy Ray responded, "I would love that sir. What do I do?"

The gentleman said, "Come down to my office on Wednesday at 5:30. You will see the sign Dr. H. V. Bailey."

Billy Ray said, "I will be there."

When they met in his office, Dr. Bailey immediately handed Billy Ray a book written in 1937 by Napoleon Hill titled, *Think and Grow Rich*. He also explained the process of positive thinking and visualization that formed the basis of the book. Dr. Bailey reiterated that one could achieve whatever one wanted, with the techniques in that book. Together, for the next few months, they studied *Think and Grow Rich* one chapter at a time. Billy Ray said he copied down lines such as, "As ye sow, so shall ye reap," and "What the mind can conceive and believe, it can achieve," and "As a man thinks in his heart, and in his soul, so is he." He said it all came down to this: "thoughts are things."

Billy Ray not only used the principles of *Think and Grow Rich* to reach his plane of success in music, he previously had applied them to the game of baseball. He said he visualized himself hitting better and more powerfully, and it worked. He stated, "I went on a home-run tear."

He then went on to say, at one point his single-minded-drive was to make it in the music business, to reach his goal, and most importantly find his purpose. He stated this drive was stronger than anything he'd ever known. It defined everything about him.

Another quote from Napoleon Hill kept running through his mind . . . "Persistence is to the character of man, as carbon is to steel." He said this was the statement that kept him going through tough times and self-doubt and motivated him to go to LA then back to Nashville . . . in short, to never give up.

Note: *Think and Grow Through Art and Music* is based on these exact set of principles and practices.

Introduction

HOW TO BENEFIT THE MOST FROM
THINK and GROW THROUGH ART and MUSIC

Success and failure are the result of thought. However, less than one percent of all people realize that our thoughts shape our lives. For the most part, we tend to believe we are limited by our circumstances or other people and conditions in which we seem to have no control. However, it is a fact that anyone, including you, can reshape your world immediately by reshaping your thinking. You will be able to prove this to yourself as you read and study the principles of success outlined in *Think and Grow Through Art and Music.*

One fundamental suggestion, I would like to point out, is to read and study this book in the order it is written. Each chapter adds to, and builds on, the principles given in the previous chapters like the links of a chain. Each one extending into and becoming a part of the principle preceding and the principle following it. It is beneficial to review each chapter as many times as necessary to understand the information enclosed. Please note, this understanding is of little use unless you apply the key word "**Action.**" I believe it's important to also pace your reading and studying, so you can give your mind time to digest and process what you have just read.

As a test, I suggest you read each chapter twice. You might be amazed at how much you pick up the second time, that you might have missed the first. When reading new material with new ideas, sometimes our mind has a tendency to wander as we continue to read words without comprehension. By reading a chapter twice, you will be able to see what I'm referring to. Please try it.

The purpose of *Think and Grow Through Art and Music* is to help guide you to become a successful musician and artist. I vowed I would not include anything in this book, unless it helped us both reach our goals. When I re-read the manuscript, I discovered scenarios, stories and specific examples that might not seem like they have hands-on-benefit, however, they contain certain concepts relating to working behind the scenes. Some of these scenarios build self-confidence, teach persistence, and strengthen your belief system.

Please have confidence in this philosophy, and embrace the fact that by putting these principles into **Action**, you will succeed and arrive at your "Plane of Success."

As you are reading, continually ask yourself—"What does this mean to me?" As you read and study, pay close attention to any and all instructions you receive, that can bring you closer to your goal. Take **Action** in following these instructions. **Action** is the key.

I have intentionally tried to write this book free of academic terms and phrases, which sometimes can become quite confusing.

Throughout this entire book, you will notice I use repetition as a teaching tool. When I say the exact statement in the exact same way, time and time again, it's because some truths do not need variation.

Is it possible you can read this book and not attain your Plane of Success? Yes.

Let's use this example to explain the how and why. Let's say you have a perfectly working camera, with perfectly working film. You take photo upon photo, however, you cannot sell a single one of them. Someone else picks up the same camera, takes photos, and sells everyone of them. Was it the cameras fault? Of course not. Could it be because you did not apply the principles you were taught when learning how to use your camera?

This example also applies to *Think and Grow Through Art and Music*. You must follow this blueprint with a *Positive Mental Attitude*, *Faith*, and *Persistence*, in order to reach your Plane of Success. These principles are sound.

If you would like to obtain an overall view of these principles, read *Think and Grow Through Art and Music* only *once*.

If you would like a more thorough understanding of these principles, read it *twice*.

If you would like to reach your Plane of Success, read it *three times*, and then again once a year until you have arrived.

1
Desire

THE STARTING POINT OF ALL ACHIEVEMENT

The First Step Toward Reaching Your Plane of Success

According to Napoleon Hill (1883–1970), *Desire* is the starting point of all achievement. The very first step is to decide exactly what it is you desire? What is your end goal? For the purpose of these instructions we will call this end goal your Plane of Success. To reach your Plane of Success you will actually need more than just desire, you will need what Dr. Hill referred to as *A Burning Desire*. A burning desire is much more than just a want. It is a passion. It starts out as a thought. From there it becomes the motivating force that drives everything about your being—everyday. You will not have a burning desire unless you have a motive that, figuratively speaking, sets you on fire.

How do you know if you have a burning desire? In your past, has some one said to you any of the following: "Don't you ever give up?" or "You sure do have tenacity." "You are determined aren't you?" "Have you always been this stubborn and passionate?" or "You sure are focused." If so, then chances are, if you look back at whatever you were seeking, you most likely had *A Burning Desire*. Now, I ask you—did you get what you were seeking? If not, did you keep pushing until there was absolutely no way you could carry on with your purpose? If so, you definitely had *A Burning Desire*.

In the original *Think and Grow Rich*, written by Napoleon Hill in 1937, he spoke of a *burning desire* as it related to success.

> "Every human being who reaches the age of understanding of the purpose of success wishes for it. Wishing will not bring success, but desiring success with a state of mind that becomes an obsession, then planning a definite way and means to acquire success, and backing these plans with persistence which does not recognize failure, will bring success."

This statement is worth reading a second time, right now!

Do you have a burning desire to become a successful musician and/or artist? You must work yourself into a white heat of desire to reach your Plane of Success. Has your desire become an obsession in which you are powerless to resist? If so, you are well on your way.

Ground Rule

I would like to pause for just a moment and share a monumental source of insight, which I refer to as a ground rule. The most important factor in this entire book is not written on these pages, however you already possess it. It's in your mind. You become what you think about. Dr. Hill's famous quote will become quite evident before you have finished studying this book: "What the mind of man can conceive and believe, it can achieve . . . with a positive mental attitude." It's your thoughts that control who and what you become. By taking possession of your mind you will become the master of your greatest enemy and your greatest friend—Yourself. For that which you think today, becomes what you are tomorrow. Whether you think you can or you think you can't, you're right either way. The only limitations you have are the ones you set up in your own mind. Yes, by understanding and accepting this "ground rule" you will learn how to control and guide your mind to lead you to your desired outcome. By reading, studying and putting into action the principles outlined in *Think and Grow Through Art and Music*, you will learn to build and organize the knowledge in your mind and guide it to the attainment of your Definite Major Purpose in life. More to follow, on this Definite Major Purpose in the next chapter.

The Origination of Desire

Where does desire originate? You know and I know that one day you either saw or heard something or someone who caught your ear. There was that "aha" moment when you said, "That's what I want to do. I want to make or be involved with music, or I want to be that type of artist." Do you remember who or what you heard? In nearly every interview I have conducted, this desire started at a very young age.

Brief History Lesson

It would take an entire book to give you the origin of music. That is not our purpose here. A very condensed version might go something like this; History tells us music had its beginning approximately 3400 years ago. The Syrians composed one of the first songs ever written. The 3400-year-old Hurrian Hymn No. 6 is the oldest known fragment of written music thus far discovered. The oldest musical composition to have survived in its entirety is a first century A.D. Greek tune known as "Seikilos Epitaph." This song was found engraved on a marble column used to mark a prestigious woman's gravesite.

If we fast-forward briefly, we see that the Medieval and Renaissance era covers approximately 500–1600 A.D., then Baroque approximately 1600–1750 (Bach), the Classical era approximately 1750–1820, then the Romantic era approximately 1810–1910. During the Renaissance and Baroque eras, there were many brilliant composers. More common-place names came from the Classical era. Three composers dominated this Classical era: Franz Joseph Hayden (1732–1809), Wolfgang Amadeus Mozart (1756–1791) and Ludwig van Beethoven (1770–1827).

Where did these *greats* draw their inspiration? We cannot all be child prodigies. History shows us even Beethoven was greatly influenced by Mozart, Bach, and Handel.

If you answered the question I posed earlier then you can pin point your exact "aha" moment. This was the onset of your desire which, I assume by now has developed into a "burning desire," hence the reason you are reading this book. In my interviews, I have been told over and over, how their desires started at an early age.

Richie Furray of Buffalo Springfield and Poco fame, said he had seen an Ozzie and Harriet show with Ricky Nelson (1940–1985) singing Be Bop Baby to a little baby in a crib, then shortly thereafter saw him playing in a high school gymnasium full of kids. He said his "aha" moment was right then as he instantly knew he was going to pursue music as a career.

Henry Gross of Sha Na Na fame, and writer of the number one song, "Shannon," said, as soon as he saw Elvis Presley (1935–1977) in *Jailhouse Rock* at a local cinema matinee, he knew music was going to be his career. His mother, who was a pianist and sang briefly with the Metropolitan Opera chorus, had inspired Henry as he was taking the obligatory piano lessons. However, that day at the matinee changed everything as he knew it. It was all guitar from that point on.

Singer-Songwriter Rodney Crowell said his father put him on his shoulders and took him to see Hank Williams (1923–1953). He said he knew right then as a young tyke, that music was his destiny.

It was basically the same scenario for Kendrick Lamar (American Rapper and Songwriter). Dr. Dre and Tupac were shooting the second California Love video. Kendrick said, "Pops had seen them and ran back to the house and got me, then put me on his neck and we stood there watching Dre and Pac in a Bentley." Right then is when Kendrick knew he could follow their lead, which of course he has taken to a new level.

I could go on. However, by now you have the idea of where desire originates. In much the same way as you were inspired by your "aha" moment, so were all of *the greats* who came before you. Just think, you will eventually become an inspiration to those much younger than you. A good many of them you will never meet and possibly they might not even exist in your lifetime.

As one of the most distinctive voices in bluegrass, John Cowan, lead singer of the New Grass Revival for seventeen years, and bass player for the Doobie Brothers said, "Pedigree is everything in an artist. Learn as much as you can about the people who came before you. Learn how they did it, why they did it, where they did it, when they did it, as well as what they did."

In the year 2000, the turn of the millennium, Sir John Eliot Gardiner, a symphony conductor, successfully persuaded his players and singers to join him on a 40,000-mile tour . . . the momentous Bach Cantata Pilgrimage. He claims he owes Sir Charles Mackerras (1925–2010), a huge debt. He said Sir Charles was one of the very few conductors he had met who was generous enough to treat his colleagues not as rivals, but as co-interpreters with whom he could exchange personal findings, hints, tricks or shared enthusiasms. He stated that over the years he would go to Sir Charles' home in St. John's Wood to discuss scores (by Handel, Mozart, Beethoven, Berlioz, Shumann, Dvorak, Martinu), or just to receive a practical lesson in whichever Janacek opera he was conducting at the time. Nearly every *great* had help and found inspiration from *greats* who have gone before them.

Rodney Crowell told me in another way. He said, "If you hear something you like, then say 'I want to play like that' or 'I want to sing like that.' Then start where you are today and practice that sound until you get it. Then your own personal style will develop from there."

Napoleon Hill provided these six steps to take, which are both definite and practical methods of turning your Desire into success. I have summarized them for your needs:

Six Keys to Success

1. Be definite about the exact Plane of Success you desire. It is not enough to just say, I want to be a successful musician. You must be exact regarding your instrument and/or the definite part you plan to play in your quest for artistic success.

2. Commit to what you are willing to give in exchange for this Plane of Success. (There is no such thing as something for nothing.)

3. Establish the exact date you intend to reach this Plane of Success. This is crucially important.

4. Create a definite plan of action, and begin at once. A goal without a plan is simply a wish without *burning desire*. Do not procrastinate, begin at once whether you are ready or not.

5. Write a clear, concise personal mission statement, denoting the Plane of Success you plan to achieve. State the time limit you are allowing yourself to achieve it, and what you intend to give in exchange for this success. Describe clearly the plan, or action steps you will take to achieve this success.

6. Read your mission statement out loud at least twice daily, once upon arising in the morning and again just before retiring at night. As you read—*See* and *Feel* and *Believe* yourself already reaching your Plane of Success.

* * *

It is important to follow these six keys to success to the letter. It is imperative to observe and follow the instructions in the sixth key. I will offer more help later on creating your mission statement. I would also like to make a brief mention that as you progress; you will need to add *Emotion* while reading your mission statement. (More on this fundamental requirement later.) It is also important to know that your exact goal and the date to achieve it, will change from time to time. This is completely normal. You may express concern today that it's impossible for you to visualize yourself as having already reached your Plane of Success before you actually arrive. This is where your Burning Desire becomes most beneficial. When your desire becomes an obsession you should have no problem convincing yourself that you will accomplish this goal. The object here is to want this Plane of Success with such intensity and determination that you completely convince yourself you will have it. By convincing yourself you will achieve your Plane of Success, you will actually be able to see yourself arriving. This picture you can see in your mind's eye is essential and will act as a guide to keep you on your pathway to your Plane of Success.

The teacher stated, "Tell me what you desire the most and I will tell you who can do the most to help you get it." The student said, "And who would that be?" The teacher replied, "Look in the mirror and you will see that person." Now did you get the entire meaning here? First you must know what you desire and define your Definite Major Purpose. Then realize you are the only one who can make it happen.

I would like to back up a moment to make sure your Definite Major Purpose and your goals are actually your desires. You cannot develop your goals around what others want, what others expect of you or even what you think others expect of you. You must set these goals for yourself. After all, they are *your* goals. What you do, you must do for yourself by following your desires and no one else's.

The Difference Between Wishing, Desiring and Believing

The following is taken from Napoleon Hill's electrifying course, "Your Right to Be Rich" from Nightingale-Conant.

The majority of people never discover the difference between wishing and believing. Nor do they recognize that there are six steps that successful people usually follow in using their mind-power for the attainment of their desires. These steps are:

1. Stop wishing for what you want from life. The vast majority of people go through life by merely wishing for things. The percentage of people who stop at wishing is estimated at seventy percent.

2. Move from wishing to *desiring*. A much smaller percentage of people develop their wishes into desires. These are estimated at ten percent.

3. Add hope to the process. A still smaller percentage of people develop their wishes and desires into hopes. These are estimated at eight percent.

4. Move from hoping to believing. A still smaller percentage of people step their mind-power up to where it becomes belief. These are estimated at six percent.

5. Move from believing to having *faith*. A much smaller percentage of people crystalize wishes, desires and hopes into belief, and then into burning desire, and finally *faith*. This percentage is estimated at four percent.

6. Achieve success by adding action to your *faith*. The smallest percentage of people take the last two steps, putting their *faith* into action by planning and acting to carry out their plans. This percentage is estimated at only two percent. As you read today, I would suggest striving to be part of this two percent.

Those who reach their Plane of Success are the ones in the last group. They recognize the powers of their minds and take possession of those powers and direct them to whatever ends they choose. To these people, the word impossible has no meaning. To them, everything they want or need is possible and they manage to get it. The only trait that differentiates them from most of the others who accept failure as their lot, is that they recognize and use their mind-power for the attainment of the things they want while the others do not.

A Story of Determination

A great warrior once faced a situation, which made it necessary for him to make a decision ensuring his success on the battlefield. He was sending his men against an army of men who outnumbered his own. He loaded his warriors into boats, sailed to the enemy's country, unloaded the soldiers and equipment, and then gave the order to burn the ships that had carried them. He then said to his men, "You see your boats going up in smoke, this means we cannot leave these shores alive unless we win. We have no choice . . . We Win Or We Perish!" They of course won.

If you expect success with your band, your instrument, your symphony, your song writing, your voice, your paintbrush or any other artistic medium, you must be willing to cut all sources of retreat. You must be willing to "Burn Your Ships." It is only by doing this that you can be sure of maintaining that state of mind known as a "burning desire." This is essential to your success in the field of art and music.

The Power of Great Dreams

"Dream lofty dreams, and as you dream, so shall you become. Your vision is the promise of what you shall one day be; your Ideal is the prophecy of what you shall at last unveil."

—JAMES ALLEN (1864–1912)

Les Paul (1915–2009), jazz, country, and blues guitarist; songwriter, luthier; inventor; and pioneer of the solid body guitar asked: "Do you remember as a child, when you were doing your chores or shoveling snow, cutting the grass or some other unpleasant task? Do you remember saying to yourself, when I grow up, I'm not going to be shoveling snow, I'm going to be playing this or writing that. This was your dream to follow! This is how *the greats* come about. So I would tell anyone to set your sights high on where you want to go in life, make up your mind you're going to succeed no matter what, then visualize yourself already there and start digging." Les told me he had the habit of always seeing himself "doing," whatever it was he longed to do.

Since you are seeking success in the field of art and music, you will be encouraged to know that this changing world in which we live, is demanding new ideas, new ways of recording, new ways of performing live, new leaders, new inventions, new methods of teaching, new methods of marketing, new books, new features for television, new ideas for music in movies, as well as new ideas for encouraging young people and helping them follow their dreams. This of course is the purpose of *Think and Grow Through Art and Music* and hopefully the reason you are reading it. As you continue to formulate in your mind your pathway to success, let no one influence you to scorn the dream. To become one of *the greats*, you must catch the spirit of those you admire, those pioneers who have gone before you. Their dreams gave the field of art and music all that it has of value and its spirit, which serves the lifeblood of our own country and your opportunity, to develop and market your talents.

A Signal from Overseas

Graham Nash (The Hollies; Crosby, Stills, Nash and Young), Officer of the Order of the British Empire, two-time Rock and Roll Hall of Fame inductee, recipient of four honorary doctorates, and Grammy Award winner, shared his story with me by saying, "It was a signal from overseas that changed my life! While growing up in England, on Sunday nights I could pick up a signal from Radio Luxembourg. I heard Buddy Holly, The Everly Brothers, Elvis Presley, Little Richard, etc. It changed my life. I could see what I wanted to be."

Now I ask you, do you remember your signal?

Rock and Roll Hall of Famer, Dave Mason (Traffic), gave me a similar response as he said, "Growing up in the United Kingdom, my first inspiration came around age fifteen, when I heard records from the United States that inspired me." His advice: "Start now, just start."

Country Music Hall of Famer, Connie Smith-Stuart (Marty Stuart), shared her story with me. She said, "When I was five years old, I was attracted to the sound of the steel guitar. I paid close attention and found it was from The Louvin Brothers on the Grand Ole Opry." In her excitement, she said, "I'm going to grow up and play The Grand Ole Opry." Of course, that is exactly what she did, many times over. She also said, "I would also advise beginners to check their motives and make sure it's God's calling for them."

Napoleon Hill said, "If the thing you wish to do is right, (*and you believe it*), go ahead and do it." Follow your dream and never mind what "*They*" say. "*They*" perhaps do not know that every failure brings with it the seed of an equivalent success. Said another way, Dr. Hill states, "Every adversity carries with it the seed of an equivalent benefit or greater." In other words when you meet with an adverse situation, a stumbling block or temporary defeat, look for the seed of an equivalent benefit or success. It's always there. It's a law of nature. Sometimes you will not see it immediately, it might take a week, a month, a year, however, it's a law of nature, like gravity, it is always there. This one statement alone, can spur you on to continue when you have been met with a temporary stumbling block.

You will learn that it takes a *Positive Mental Attitude* in order to convert adversities, defeats and failures into assets. It seems to have been intended that everyone should experience adversity as part of nature's method of disciplining all people to learn how to take possession of their own mind. Once you learn that adversities do carry benefits, you will acquire the habit of looking for that seed of an equivalent benefit or greater.

I asked Henry Gross, "Speaking now to a younger person who has the desire to become a professional musician, what is the one thing you would say to him/her to encourage them to follow their dream?" Henry's reply, "It's the creative process you must deeply love. If you can imagine yourself doing anything else . . . then go do it." He also wrote this song in the mid 1980s. His words still resonate true today.

What You Dream

Nobody knows what you can do
No one can say not even you
Might like to teach or race a car
Be a detective or a movie star

What you dream is what you get
Anything is possible your time is yet, to come
Close your eyes and drift away but don't forget
What you dream is what you get

Don't need a match to light this fire
Just need a burning desire
You write the book, make your own breaks
Imagination is all it takes

What you dream is what you get
Anything is possible your time is yet, to come
Close your eyes and drift away but don't forget
What you dream is what you get

When the night is gone
The dream goes on and on

What you dream is what you get
Anything is possible your time is yet, to come
Close your eyes and drift away but don't forget
What you dream is what you get

Can you imagine all the dreams this world has had? Bill Gates, a computer. Thomas Edison, a light bulb. Les Paul and Leo Fender, an electric guitar. The Wright Brothers, a flying machine. Henry Ford, a horseless carriage. Marconi dreamed of harnessing the intangible forces of the ether, hence the radio. Evidence that these dreamers did not dream in vain, and may be found in every corner of our world. This world is filled with an abundance of opportunity that the dreamers of the past never knew existed.

How to Launch Your Dreams

You must first have a dream before you can make it come true. To kick-start your dreams you must have your burning desire buried in your heart. Dreams are not born from having lack of ambition and laziness.

To follow through with your dreams, you must display great enthusiasm and confidence . . . you must believe. "Dreams set the stage, but it's Action that completes the performance."

Remember that most who succeed in life get off to a rough start, and overcome many heart breaking struggles before they "arrive." So often this "arrival" comes right at the tail end of some crisis through which they are introduced to their "other selves." This other self does not understand these two words—giving up. It does not recognize failure in any form.

O. Henry (1862–1910) an American writer who wrote hundreds of short stories about common life in America, discovered his genius while incarcerated.

Charles Dickens (1812–1870) a Victorian author, was inspired by the grief of losing the love of his life. He is widely known for his unforgettable epic stories and vivid characters and is one of the world's truly prolific novelists.

Helen Keller (1880–1968) was stricken by an illness at age two, that left her deaf, mute, and blind. This misfortune did not stop her in gaining recognition as a political activist and a renowned American author. Despite this adversity she persevered in writing her name in the pages of history. Her entire life has served as evidence that "No one ever is defeated until defeat has been accepted by them, as a reality."

Ludwig van Beethoven, a German composer and pianist, was deaf. John Milton, the famous seventeenth century poet and civil servant for the commonwealth of England, was blind. However, they both became *greats* because they dreamed and translated their dreams into organized thought.

Stevie Wonder, a child prodigy, accomplished American singer, songwriter, pianist, music producer and multi-instrumentalist, who went blind at six weeks of age, said, "Just because a man lacks the use of his eyes, doesn't mean he lacks vision."

Napoleon Hill continues as he says there is a difference between merely *wishing* for something and being ready to receive it. No one is ready for anything until believing he or she can acquire it. The state of mind must have Belief, not mere hope or just wishing. Open mindedness is essential. Closed minds do not inspire *faith*, courage or belief. Remember, no more effort is required to aim high in life, than is required to accept misery and failure. The same amount of energy is used, so why not aim high?

Don't Let Them Tell You No

Madame Ernestine Schumann-Heink (1861–1936) has the before and after life of a fairytale story. Born in poverty, considered plump and awkward on stage, she started singing in public at age fifteen. She was constantly teased and called "Tiny" and "Topsy" due to her size. Early in her career, Mme. Schumann-Heink visited the director of the Vienna Court Opera, to have him test her voice. But he did not test it. After taking one look at this awkwardly, poorly-dressed girl, he exclaimed, none too gently, "With such a face, and no personality at all, how can you ever expect to succeed in opera? My good child, give up the idea. Buy a sewing machine and go to work. You can n*ever be a singer!*"

Obviously the director of the Vienna Court Opera knew much about the technique of singing, however, he knew little about the power of desire. Especially when this desire assumes the proportion of an obsession. If he had understood more regarding the "power of desire," he would not have made the mistake of condemning genius without giving it an opportunity. Madame Ernestine Schumann-Heink went on to be known as one of the greatest contraltos of her era, and perhaps of all time.

Again, do not listen to what *"They Say."*

Now, how can you, right there where you sit today, harness and use this magic power of desire? Keep reading and believing and your desire will eventually become a burning desire in which no force can possibly extinguish. Here is another profound statement from Napoleon Hill; "Through some strange and powerful principle of 'Mental Chemistry,' which she has never divulged, nature wraps up in the impulse of strong desire 'that something' which recognizes no such word as impossible, and accepts no such reality as failure." This is another sentence worth reading a second time, right now!

Chapter 1 QR Code Recap
Desire   Video Duration 9:15 minutes

This QR Code excerpt was created from "Your Right To Be Rich" series Chappell Enterprises L.L.C. and The Napoleon Hill Foundation.

www.naphill.org/tgtam/chapter-1/   Available at: yourrighttoberich.com

2
Faith

The Second Step Toward Reaching
Your Plane of Success

*"Faith is to believe what you do not yet see; the reward for this is to
see what you believe."*

—St. Augustine

It takes *faith* to believe that the dreams you dare to dream really can
come true. *Faith* is the ability to believe in yourself and your dream
when no one else does. It is the invisible force that allows us to with-
stand the many obstacles that cross our paths. How far you go toward
fulfilling your dream will be determined largely by the extent to which
you develop this invaluable substance we call "faith." *Faith* is a state of
mind in which you clear your mind of all negative ideas and condition
it for the in flowing of *Infinite Intelligence.*

Faith comes in all forms. When I asked Pat Boone (American
singer, composer, actor, and motivational speaker), if he had had any
significant help or encouragement along the way, he said, "It was Bing

Crosby and Frank Sinatra, who gave me *faith* in myself, when they said—'Pat Boone is the great white hope—he sings rock and roll, however he can also sing ballads and good music and maybe he can change the picture for the better.'—This is when I started to believe in myself and have the *faith* and courage to push ahead and not give up."

Dr. Hill stated, "*Faith* is the head chemist of the mind. When *faith* is blended with the vibration of thought, the subconscious mind instantly picks up the vibration, translates it into its spiritual equivalent, and transmits it to *Infinite Intelligence*, as in the case of prayer. The emotions of *faith*, *love* and *sex* are the most powerful of all the major positive emotions. When the three are blended, they have the effect of 'coloring' the vibration of thought in such a way that it instantly reaches the subconscious mind, where it is changed into its spiritual equivalent, which is the only form that induces a response from *Infinite Intelligence*."

If you are not familiar with the term *Infinite Intelligence* or *Universal Intelligence*, it will be explained in detail in the upcoming chapters, and throughout this entire book.

Love and *faith* are related to the spiritual side of man. *Sex* is purely biological and related only to the physical. The mixing or blending of these three emotions has the effect of opening a direct line of communication between the finite thinking of man and *Infinite Intelligence*.

Please note that anxiety, negativity and worry, will subdue your ability to have *faith* in whatever you are anxious or worrying about. Anxiety and worry can counter-act your own self-confidence and *faith* in yourself as well as your feelings of being worthy. You will need to learn and put into practice the qualities of self-confidence and *faith* to achieve your Plane of Success.

It has been said, "Faith is the fuel that pushes us when our minds are worn out and our muscles are tired, however the spirit in our hearts are still on fire." We have *faith* in electrical current but we cannot see it. We flip the light switch having *faith* the light will come on, yet we cannot see the driving force that makes it so.

How to Develop Faith

Let's take a look at *faith*, as it relates to our subconscious mind through the power and practice of Autosuggestion. There is so much to be said in this arena that I could write an entire book on the subject of Faith, Autosuggestion and the Power of the Subconscious. Here is a statement that will give you a better understanding of just how important the principle of Autosuggestion plays in reaching your Plane of Success. Dr. Hill states, "Faith is a state of mind, which may be induced, or created, by affirmation or repeated instructions to the subconscious mind, through the principle of Autosuggestion."

By following the instructions in the upcoming chapter on Autosuggestion and the chapter on the Subconscious Mind you will gain a powerful skill. By repeated suggestions, mixed with emotion, you will eventually convince your subconscious mind that you Do Believe and you Will Receive, that which you ask for. In turn your subconscious will act upon your belief and pass back to you in the form of "Faith" followed by definite plans for reaching your Plane of Success. Dr. Hill further explains: "*Faith* is a state of mind which you may develop at will, after you have mastered the thirteen principles. It is a state of mind which develops voluntarily, through the application and use of these principles. Bold repetition and affirmation of orders to your subconscious mind is the only known method of voluntary development of the virtue of *faith*."

Once again, consider this statement: *All thoughts, which have been emotionalized and mixed with faith, begin immediately to translate themselves into their physical equivalent or counterpart. This in turn will help boost you to your Plane of Success.*

The length of time you must keep conditioning your mind by repetition before you start to see positive results, depends almost entirely on the amount of *faith*, *emotion*, and *enthusiasm* you place behind your words. Without these three factors, these principles work very slowly.

The good news about these principles is the fact that you can't be cheated. The law of compensation will make sure you receive payment or rewards for every positive action you take. Even the Bible states, "As a man sows, so also shall he reap."

One disturbing facet of these principles and entire philosophy is the fact that you will never again be able to justify any failures or temporary defeats by using alibis. You will never again be able to truthfully claim that life never gave you the opportunity to succeed. You will learn that you are in control of your mind and therefore you have potential power to change any circumstances in your life to benefit your Definite Major Purpose in life.

Here are two ideas that are inseparably associated with *faith*. First, *faith* requires persistent action backed by a Definite Major Purpose. Second, a strong sense of purpose and strong motives clears your mind of most doubts, fears and other negative attitudes. These must be removed to allow *faith* to operate. When you desire something and pursue that desire actively, you will soon find that your mind is automatically prepared for the guidance of *faith*.

Before this state of mind known as *faith* will produce practical results, it must be expressed in some form of action. All the *faith* in the world will not bring about results unless you take action.

It's important here to start digesting this most important fact regarding Autosuggestion and your Subconscious Mind. Your subconscious mind does not know the difference between positive input and negative input. It cannot differentiate between the two. If you feed it negative suggestions, it will do its best to bring negative results, just as by feeding it positive suggestions, it brings positive results. This is especially important when faced with adversity. If you allow those thoughts surrounding the adverse situation to take root, they will blossom. Equally so when you block them out and replace them with 100% positive thoughts, then these positive thoughts take root and begin to blossom.

Faith Formula
HOW TO DEVELOP, EMPLOY AND MAINTAIN FAITH

1. Know what you want and believe that you can and will get it.
2. Express gratitude many times daily for having already received what you want.
3. Keep your mind open for hunches, and when you are inspired for action, move at once.
4. When defeat comes, accept it as nothing more than a challenge to keep on trying.
5. Develop a burning desire as the starting point of *Faith*.
6. Believe in yourself and act, and keep on acting.
7. Whenever doubt creeps in treat it for what it is, a doubt. Believe your beliefs and doubt your doubts.
8. Start where you are with what you have, knowing that what you have is plenty enough.

How Faith Overcame Adversity

The following are a few examples of how *faith* conquered adverse situations. Situations, in which the majority of people would have given up.

Gypsy music genius DjAngo Reinhardt (1910–1953), met with challenge at an early age. He started learning to play music as a young boy, starting with violin and then moving on to banjo and finally guitar. When he was 18, tragedy struck. He and his wife were living in a caravan selling imitation flowers to supplement his meager musician's income. He accidentally knocked over a candle on his way to bed. The caravan burst into flames, destroying all his personal belongings and leaving him with first and second degree burns over the entire left side of his body. As a result his leg and the third and fourth fingers on his left hand were completely paralyzed. Doctors told him they would need to amputate his leg and he would never play another stringed instrument.

DjAngo repeated daily that he had *Faith* in the fact that he would walk again and he visualized himself actually walking. Reinhardt refused the surgery and with the aid of a cane was able to walk again within a year. While his fingers never recovered, the doctors were also wrong about his music career. As it happened, learning to play guitar again may also have saved his life. He ended up being detained in France during World War II. He said that due to their respect for music, a handful of jazz-loving Nazis ensured his safety despite the fact that thousands of Gypsies were murdered under Nazi-occupied territories. He went on to be one of the greatest musicians in the twentieth century.

Tony Iommi of Black Sabbath had a dream of being a rock star. He had some talent, however was from a very poor family, which forced him to work at a sheet metal factory rather than chase his dream. He was just starting to gain recognition as a musician, when on what was to be his last day of factory work, Iommi unfortunately severed the tips of the middle and ring finger on his right hand. As a leftie this meant fretting was nearly impossible. He was contemplating on giving up, however after his boss told him about DjAngo Reinhardt's mishap, Tony was soon trying to master guitar again. He tried playing right handed, to no avail. He went onto develop prosthetic fingertips using plastic, covered in leather. Because the prostate fingers weren't as tough as the real thing, Iommi started using lighter strings and de-tuning them so the tension would be lowered. Suddenly this dark, deep sound of heavy-metal was born solely as a technique to work around injury. Tony Iommi is recorded in the history books as number 86 on Rolling Stone's "100 Guitar Greats of All Time," and number 1 in Guitar World's "100 Greatest Metal Guitarist of All Times." Tony graduated from sheet-metal to heavy-metal by believing that if DjAngo could overcome his challenge, then so could he.

Jerry Garcia (1942–1995) acclaimed bandleader of the Grateful Dead, accidentally had his middle finger severed during a wood-chopping incident at age five. This did not detour him from developing one of the largest cult-like entourage of fans in the world of music. They gained a following of millions, who fittingly called themselves Deadheads and were a major part of the psychedelic-counter-culture of the 1960s. His most famous quote, "Let there be songs to fill the air."

Chet Baker (1929–1988), the acclaimed jazz trumpeter, had all his front teeth knocked out while trying to score heroin. After being fitted for dentures, he learned to play the trumpet for the second time. If you've never played a woodwind or brass instrument, this might not seem difficult, but the reality is that these instruments require a precise use of the lips, teeth, and facial muscles to be able to create a distinctive sound. It took him eight years to relearn. Most would have given up, however he said he always had *faith* that he would play again and even better than ever. In 1973 he went on to join Dizzy Gillespie (1917–1993), and then play a reunion concert with saxaphonist Gerry Mulligan at Carnegie Hall in 1974.

Rick Allen, the drummer for Def Leppard, tragically had his right arm severed in a car accident. He got to the hospital very quickly and was able to have it reattached. It was eventually amputated due to infection. Most drummers would have given up, but he had *faith* he would play again. He and his band mates met with an engineer who designed a drum kit that could be played with only one arm and both feet. Rick continued to play and tour with the band, which subsequently went on to reach its most commercially successful phase. He is known to his fans as "The Thunder God."

I sum these cases up in one word: Persistence. *Faith* conquers all.

History is filled with stories and lessons on adversity. These are just a few examples to open your mind to the many possibilities available to you even after being faced with what some might consider, career devastating setbacks. Remember—A setback is just a set-up for a comeback—When you are faced with disappointment and remain in *faith*, you will realize you can still grow and reach your Plane of Success.

This will help you become stronger therefore realizing . . . *faith* helps you grow, and growing builds your *faith*. It has been said that *faith* is like taking the first step, even when you can't see the staircase. It keeps your dreams alive. To understand and achieve anything requires *faith, belief in yourself, vision, hard work, determination,* and *dedication*. Remember, all things are possible for those who believe.

Let's take a closer look at what Dr. Hill set forth regarding *faith* and the role it plays in bringing forth your Plane of Success. "Have *faith* in yourself: *Faith* in the Infinite. *Faith* is the 'external elixir,' which gives life, power and action to the impulse of thought! *Faith* is the starting point in every Plane of Success. *Faith* is the basis of all 'miracles' and all 'mysteries' that cannot be analyzed by the rules of science! *Faith* is the only known antidote for Failure! *Faith* is the element, the 'chemical,' which when mixed with prayer, gives one direct communication with *Infinite Intelligence. Faith* is the element, which transforms the ordinary vibration of thought, created by the finite mind of man, into the spiritual equivalent. *Faith* is the only agency through which the cosmic force of *Infinite Intelligence* can be harnessed and used by man."

Les Paul said that he and Mary Ford rose to number one in their days because they had *faith* and confidence that they could, and would be, number one. He said their *faith* pushed them to work day and night and harder and longer than others or they would not have attained their dream. He said to never lose *faith* in yourself. *Faith* doesn't cost a thing; it's completely free.

As country great Martina McBride said, "*Faith* that it's not always in your hands or things don't always go the way you planned, but you have to have *faith* that there is a plan for you, and you must follow your heart and believe in yourself no matter what."

Thus far we've touched slightly on desire, faith and guiding your subconscious mind through Autosuggestion. Let's take a deeper look into how your dream, or seed of an idea can be planted in your mind. The information is easily conveyed; any idea, plan, or purpose may be placed in the mind *through repetition of thought.* This is why you were instructed to write out a statement of your Definite Major Purpose, or your definite chief aim, commit it to memory, and repeat it, loudly in *Audible Words,* day after day, until these vibrations of sound have reached your subconscious mind.

Now taking an inventory of your mental assets and liabilities, you may discover your greatest weakness is lack of self-confidence. This can be overcome by Autosuggestion, also called self-talk. Dr. Hill gives us these Five Affirmations as a formula for self-confidence so that you can overcome the lack of self-confidence.

Self-Confidence Formula

First: I know that I have the ability to achieve the object of my Definite Major Purpose in life; therefore I demand of myself persistent continuous action toward its attainment, and I here and now promise to render such action.

Second: I realize the dominating thoughts of my mind will eventually reproduce themselves in outward, physical action, and gradually transform themselves into physical reality; therefore I will concentrate on my thoughts for thirty minutes daily, upon the task of thinking of the person I intend to become, thereby creating in my mind a clear mental picture.

Third: I know through the principle of Autosuggestion, any desire that I personally hold in my mind will eventually seek expression through some practical means of attaining the object behind it; therefore I will devote 10 minutes daily to demanding of myself the development of *self-confidence.*

Fourth: I have clearly written down a description of my definite chief aim in life, and I will never stop trying, until I have developed sufficient self-confidence for its attainment.

Fifth: I fully realize that no Plane of Success or position can long endure, unless built upon truth and justice; therefore, I will engage in no transaction that will not benefit all whom it affects. I will succeed by attracting to myself the force I wish to use, and the cooperation of other people. I will induce others to serve me, because of my willingness to serve others. I will eliminate hatred, envy, jealousy, selfishness, and cynicism, by developing love for all humanity, because I know that a negative attitude toward others can never bring about my Plane of Success. I will cause others to believe in me, because I believe in them, and in myself.

I will sign my name to this formula, commit it to memory, and repeat it twice a day, with full *faith* that it will gradually influence my thoughts and actions so that I will become more self-reliant in reaching my Plane of Success.

To further enhance your self-confidence, Dr. Hill went on to explain: "Back of this formula is a *law of nature*, which no man has been able to explain. The name by which one calls this law is unimportant. The important fact is that *It Works* for the glory and success of mankind, *If* used constructively. Likewise if used destructively, it will bring destruction. All impulses of thought have a tendency to clothe themselves in their physical equivalent."

Definite Major Purpose

Let's take a closer look at the meaning of number one, in the self-confidence formula. The three words—Definite Major Purpose—are monumental. Along with desire, a Definite Major Purpose is also said to be the starting point of all achievement. Your Definite Major Purpose is the why of your entire life and the reason for your existence.

It's hard to realize and fathom that ninety-eight percent of the people on this planet are drifting aimlessly through life without ever giving any consideration to the work they are best suited. They have no Definite Major Purpose. Going back in the history of this book, it was this realization that inspired Andrew Carnegie to influence over five-hundred American leaders to collaborate in the organization of these principles of success.

You are hereby encouraged to ponder and find your Definite Major Purpose in life and use the principles you will learn in this book to always keep you on a path toward your purpose.

You are encouraged from this day forward, to resolve that you will accept nothing less than your Definite Major Purpose in life. You can be anything you want in this life, if you have the *belief* and *faith* in yourself and you are willing to put in whatever work and sacrifices are needed.

As I stated above, your Definite Major Purpose is the why of your life and the reason for your existence. It's imperative that you understand this next statement. There is a difference between your purpose and your goals. Yes, they sound quite similar, however your purpose is never achieved, but is lived out. The reason you have goals is to focus your effort on achieving a desired need and to keep you on your pathway toward your Definite Major Purpose.

Think and Grow Through Art and Music will aid you in setting goals to help lead you to your Definite Major Purpose in life. There are many advantages to choosing your Definite Major Purpose. One of the most beneficial is the fact that your mind will become alerted to opportunities that will help you achieve your objectives as they present themselves in your everyday life. If you know what you want you are more apt to recognize it when you see it. An example: You run into a friend or an associate, during your conversation he or she casually mentions something that might be in direct correlation with your Definite Major Purpose. You immediately ask them to repeat or elaborate on what they said. This could prove to be a great benefit to you. Without being definite about your purpose you might not have realized the importance of what was being said. It's the difference between drifting and knowing where you are going. When you concentrate on your Definite Major Purpose, your mind not only recognizes opportunity related to your Definite Major Purpose, it also fosters the courage needed to act upon those opportunities. Another significant advantage in choosing your Definite Major Purpose is the ability to reach decisions. Successful people make decisions quickly and change them slowly, if at all. Just the opposite is true with those who fail; they make decisions slowly and change them quite often without much consideration.

Remember I mentioned 98% of the people on this planet drift aimlessly. Do you think this could be due to the fact that they are unable to make decisions?

As I have mentioned earlier, the subconscious mind cannot distinguish between constructiveness, or positive thoughts, and destructiveness, or negative thoughts. It will translate into reality the negative which is driven by fear, just as easily as it will translate into reality, the positive driven by *faith*, *courage*, and *hope*.

Exactly as electricity can power an entire building and city, it can also take a human life if used improperly. Such is life with Autosuggestion. If used properly, it will bring the Plane of Success you desire, however, if driven by fear and negativity, it can bring total chaos and failure.

Dr. Hill put it this way; "If you fill your mind with fear, doubt and unbelief in your ability to connect with and use the forces of *Infinite Intelligence*, the law of Autosuggestion will take this spirit of unbelief and use it as a pattern by which your subconscious mind will translate it into its physical equivalent." In other words again, negativity breeds negativity.

He also used this analogy: It's like the wind which carries one ship east and one ship west, the law of Autosuggestion will bring you up to your Plane of Success or pull you down. It's all according to the way you set your sails—Positive thoughts bring positive results, every time.

The poet Walter D. Wintle wrote these words which sum up this topic quite nicely:

Thinking (The Man Who Thinks He Can)

"If you think you are beaten, you are.
If you think you dare not, you don't
If you like to win, but you think you can't
It's almost certain you won't."

"If you think you'll lose, you're lost
For out in the world we find,
Success begins with ones own will—
It's all in the state of mind."

"If you think you are outclassed, you are
You've got to think high to rise.
You've got to be sure of yourself before
You can even win the prize."

"Life's battles don't always go
To the stronger or faster man
But sooner or later the one who wins
Is the one Who Thinks He Can."

A Master Musician Is Sleeping

Do you realize that inside your brain, at this exact moment, a master musician or artist could be sleeping? Yes, the seed was planted long ago, however, it must be aroused and put into action and allowed to grow. Imagine a master musician playing a beautiful piano concerto, or a genius plucking the strings of a guitar bringing forth the sound of happiness. Imagine a horn player taking you down a new avenue you have never traveled, or a painting washing away the dust on your soul through visual communication. These visions can wake up that sleeping seed in your brain and arouse these newly learned "vibrations of thought" to help create your own genius in reaching your goals. This last phrase is monumental and worth reading again: These visions can wake up that sleeping seed in your brain and arouse these newly learned "vibrations of thought" to create your own genius in reaching your goals.

Thelonious Monk (1917–1982), one of the most covered jazz composers of all time, didn't come into the mainstream until 1957, when he was 40. He really didn't reach his Plane of Success until 1963, at age 46, with his dynamic landmark release of his album *Monks Dream*.

Leonard Cohen (1934–2016), Canadian Singer-Songwriter, Poet, Author, and Lifetime Grammy Achievement Award Winner, was 33 in 1967 when he entered the starlight. However, it was 17 years later when he finally reached his Plane of Success with his highly covered recording of "Hallelujah."

Sheryl Crow did not have a hit until she was 32, after working as a schoolteacher, singing as a jingle-singer, and as a back-up vocalist (for Michael Jackson and Stevie Wonder).

Bill Withers served in the U.S. Navy for nine years and worked on a factory assembly line, before reaching his Plane of Success at age 32 with "Ain't No Sunshine."

Pharrell Williams didn't reach his Plane of Success until he wrote and sang "Happy" at age 40.

Andrea Bocelli was diagnosed with congenital glaucoma soon after his birth, which left him partially blind. At age 12 he was struck in the head while tending goal during a soccer game and unfortunately lost all his vision. This impairment, however, did not cause him to lose sight of his vision to become a world-class tenor. With dedication, devotion and confidence, at age 41 he finally reached his Plane of Success and emerged as one of the greatest talents in the world.

Leonardo Da Vinci (1452–1519) didn't paint his first masterpiece, *The Last Supper*, until he was 49 years old. Up to that point he was considered a failure.

Susan Boyle was deprived of oxygen at birth long enough to cause mild brain damage. She became a household name at age 47, when her first album sold a million copies in six weeks.

History is filled with successful artists and musicians, who reached their Plane of Success, despite age and/or challenges. Every one of these examples has something in common. They all had a sleeping genius lying inside their brains. Now I ask you, when will yours awaken?

Dr. Hill also makes note of one of his discoveries by saying, "It is a known fact that the emotion of love is closely akin to the state of mind known as *faith*, and for this reason, love comes very near to translating one's thought impulses into their spiritual equivalent." He discovered that behind nearly every successful person there was a man or woman's love. Hence the old idiom, "Behind every good man is a good woman" and vice-versa.

Let us now examine one of the foremost examples of *faith* ever displayed.

Mahatma Gandhi (1869–1948) was an astute political campaigner who fought for Indian Independence from British Rule, and for the rights of the poor people in India. Employing nonviolent, civil disobedience, Gandhi led India to independence and inspired movement for civil rights and freedom across the world. He displayed one of the most astounding examples of *faith* known to Modern civilization. He demonstrated and wielded more potential power than any man living in his time, despite the fact that he had no money, no battleships, no tanks, no soldiers, nor other ammunition of warfare. He had no home, he did not own a suit of clothes, and he had no financial means, nonetheless, he did have power. How did he come about this great power? How did he get two-hundred-million minds to think like his? There is only one answer, *faith*. Gandhi transplanted *faith* into the minds of his followers.

In closing, when you mix *Faith* with what you will learn in the next chapter on Autosuggestion, it will guide and strengthen your ability to use the power of your subconscious mind. We are now making considerable progress and I get more excited for you as every chapter closes.

Chapter 2 QR Code Recap

Faith   Video Duration 9:29 minutes

This QR Code excerpt was created from "Your Right To Be Rich" series Chappell Enterprises L.L.C. and The Napoleon Hill Foundation

www.naphill.org/tgtam/chapter-2/   Available at: yourrighttoberich.com

---

3

Autosuggestion

The Third Step Toward Reaching Your Plane of Success

In this chapter you will learn the fundamental importance of mastering the technique called "Autosuggestion." Whether you realize it or not, you have probably been using Autosuggestion techniques your entire life. For example: Have you ever told yourself you need to get up at 5:30 a.m. so that you can catch a plane? Then you wake up at 5:25 only to realize you did not really need to set your alarm to alert you at 5:30.

This was you using your God-given talent of Autosuggestion to influence your subconscious mind to wake you on time. It's almost as if your subconscious mind was watching the clock. If this can be accomplished with just one thought the night before a flight, just think what you can accomplish with repeated affirmations over a period of time. Autosuggestion techniques are used in meditation, relaxation, sleeping and any number of practices used by humans. It is a form of self-talk or self-suggestion. Some even use it *unconsciously,* in a way that could just possibly have a negative effect. An example might be—a person might talk everyday about being sick and tired. It's no wonder they soon lack energy and feel lethargic. Some think of Autosuggestion as a "New Age" term or a power used only by hypnotists. Some believe it to be non-Christian or anti-Christ. Let's take a look at one definition for Autosuggestion: "A process of suggestion in which a person unconsciously supplies or consciously attempts to supply a means of influencing his own behavior or beliefs." Another definition: "The process by which a person induces self-acceptance of an opinion, belief or plan of action."

Dr. Hill explained: "Autosuggestion is a term, which applies to all suggestion, and all self-administered stimuli that reach one's mind through the five senses." Autosuggestion is self-talk. As we noted above and in chapter two, this self-talk can take on the form of positivity with constructive natures, or negativity with destructive natures.

"Like the wind that carries one ship east and the other west,
    the law of Autosuggestion will lift you up or pull you down—
    according to the way you set your sails."

You are in control of this great power. No one else can control your thoughts, however, some would like to try. Think of a very controlling person and how they try to influence you to think exactly like them or try to sway you one way or another. How do you control your own thoughts? Do you say something to yourself like, "I do not agree with what so and so says and therefore, I'm going to continue to remain steadfast with my own God-given thoughts." This is Autosuggestion as you are, in essence telling yourself how to think.

Nature has built mankind so that we have absolute control over the information that reaches our subconscious mind, through the five senses. This does not mean man is always in control of his own thoughts. Sometimes they are guided by fear and doubt. This explains why so many people go through life without ever finding their Plane of Success. You are on the threshold of reaching yours. Let's look at this in one more light before we thrust forth on your threshold.

If we liken our mind to a fertile valley of rich black soil, we know it will grow whatever we plant. Ergo, if we plant weeds; it will grow weeds. If we plant seeds of a more desirable crop or fruit, then it will produce more desirable crop or fruit.

Autosuggestion is the department or commission in control, through which you may feed your subconscious mind either seeds of a positive or negative nature. What do you want growing in your garden?

Ok, let's see how to plant your garden. You were given some instructions in the chapter on Desire. One such instruction was to read your mission statement out loud at least twice a day. Once upon rising and especially when retiring. You were instructed to see and feel yourself already in possession and of having already reached your Plane of Success. By practicing this faithfully you are communicating your goal, or the Plane of Success you desire, directly to your subconscious mind in the truest meaning of absolute *Faith*. By repeating this process day in and day out, you are voluntarily creating thought habits, that are beneficial in transmuting your desire in reaching your Plane of Success.

I repeat many principles over and over throughout this philosophy of success. It's as Mr. Don Green, CEO of The Napoleon Hill Foundation told me one day, "I learned my ABC's, however, I did not learn them the first time, I had to keep repeating them over and over. Through repetition, I finally learned them." Therefore, I feel it beneficial for you to go back now to the six steps we outlined in Chapter Two. Read them again, slowly.

Remember, when you are reading your mission statement out loud so you can achieve your Plane of Success, that just the mere reading of the words is of little or no consequence—unless you color them with emotion and put *feeling* into your words. This sentence is worth reading again, and again. For example, one way to accomplish this might be for you to practice the following. When you are visualizing, or seeing yourself already in possession of your Plane of Success—feel the joy, feel the happiness—see others around you smiling and how happy you are now that you have brought your dream into a reality. Capture that feeling of joy and happiness as you see yourself performing your artistic endeavor. Emotion is a key player used in convincing yourself, you will accomplish that which you are feeding into your subconscious mind on a daily basis. Your subconscious mind recognizes and acts only upon thoughts that have been well blended with emotion and feeling. The lack of understanding of this major principle, is the main reason the majority of people who try to apply the principle of Autosuggestion do not get desirable results.

Just plain, unemotional words do not, and will not, influence the subconscious mind. Again, you will not reach your subconscious mind with spoken words or thoughts, until they have been saturated and emotionalized with belief.

Do not give up or become discouraged if you are not in complete control of your thoughts and emotions the first few times you try. You must remain steadfast and have *faith* that you will be able to guide your thoughts with emotion. There is no such thing as something for nothing. You cannot cheat even if you wanted to. First, you must have *faith* that what you are being taught is 100% factual. You must believe these principles are valid; second, you must never, under any circumstances, give up. It's the old saying, "Quitters never win, and winners never quit." You must remain steadfast and know with your entire being you will reach your Plane of Success in due time. You can now see how important the principle of *faith* plays and fits together in this formula for success. Your ability to influence your subconscious mind is everlasting persistence in applying these principles. You and you alone must ask yourself, "Is my Plane of Success worth the effort and dedication to these principles that I must practice daily in order to attain it?"

Backwards with Bruno

Bruno Mars (American Singer-songwriter, multi-instrumentalist, record producer, and dancer) made this statement regarding visualization: "You have to envision the life you want, and then go backwards. I have always seen where I wanted to be, now I am backtracking to get there."

In other words, Bruno projected in his mind where he was going and what he wanted to be. He then took the necessary steps which included hard work and dedication leading him to his vision and Plane of Success.

Your ability to practice Autosuggestion will greatly depend on your commitment and your capacity to concentrate upon your desire, until your desire, becomes a burning obsession. Do you believe you can accomplish your dream? Can you see yourself already in possession of your dream? If so, you are well on your way to attainment.

As I mentioned above, your success in using Autosuggestion and your ability to reach and influence your subconscious mind will greatly depend on your ability to concentrate. In other words you need to become "The Supreme Commander of your Mind."

If your goal is to learn as much as you can in reaching your Plane of Success; then strengthening your power of concentration is not just an option, it is a necessity. There are several ways to strengthen your concentration. One proven method is to "stay curious." The more curious you become about the world pertaining to your Plane of Success, the greater your stamina will become regarding concentration.

William James (1842–1910), the great American philosopher and psychologist, gave us a very simple experiment to explain how *staying curious* in regards to reaching your Plane of Success, can prolong your ability to concentrate and stay focused. Let me explain: Try to stare steadfastly at a dot on a sheet of paper or a dot on the wall. You will eventually become aware that one of two things occurs. Either your field of vision has become blurred so that you see nothing distinct at all or else you have involuntarily ceased to look at the dot in question, and are looking at something else.

Now the test: if you look at the dot again and start asking yourself questions like, how big is it, how far away is it, what exact color or shade of color is it; in other words by staying curious, you will be able to concentrate and stay focused. This technique will help you strengthen your ability to concentrate on every aspect needed in reaching your Plane of Success.

Charles Darwin (1809–1882) was a master of this concept. His contemporaries marveled at his ability to spend an entire day just staring at animals and plants. Darwin's secret was his undaunting curiosity, he would discover more and more about a single object by homing in on various details, examining it in different ways and asking himself new questions.

Dr. Hill uses an example of playing a legitimate "trick" on your subconscious mind, by *making it believe* because you believe, that you must reach your goal. You trick your subconscious by visualizing yourself already having reached your Plane of Success. You can see yourself being or doing whatever it is you desire. This is when you tell your subconscious mind that it must hand over to you a practical plan so you can acquire your Plane of Success.

Take the thought in the preceding sentence and introduce it to your imagination. Now watch what your imagination will do to create practical plans through your burning desire, to boost you on your way to reaching your Plane of Success.

Please pay particular attention to this next instruction, as it is monumental in understanding this process of receiving thoughts or impulses from your subconscious. Do not wait for your subconscious to hand over an exact outline, before visualizing yourself already in possession or position regarding your Plane of Success. As you see and feel yourself having reached your goal, your subconscious mind, little by little will start to give you your needed directions. Be prepared, as

suddenly, when you least expect it, you will be hit with an "inspiration" or a "flash," a thought that seems to come from nowhere. Eventually the subconscious mind takes over these obsessional desires. It
then hands back plans, to the conscious mind, in the form of ideas.
These ideas flash into your mind at unexpected moments. It is this
burst or startling inspiration that makes you ask "Where did that
come from?" It is actually appearing through your "sixth sense." This
is where hunches and intuitions come from. When your thoughts are
mixed with a burning desire and you are repeating your mission statement out loud, you are actually connecting with *Infinite Intelligence.*
Infinite Intelligence will bring you answers enveloped in your sixth
sense. When this *flash* or *inspiration* hits, you are liable to say, "Of
course, why didn't I think of this before?"

On more than one occasion, I have had students, or those I had
been teaching these principles to, call me in the middle of the night,
overly excited, with these exact words, "I've Got It!" Of course being
sound asleep, I would ask, "Got what?" Their answer, "I now have the
solution for what I need to do to achieve my Plane of Success. I now
know exactly what to do next." Due to their excitement, I found myself
excited for them and in most cases could not go back to sleep myself.

Now be prepared as you receive directions from *Infinite Intelligence*
and keep an open mind to the fact that these instructions may not be
the final set of steps to take. Sometimes your Plane of Success might
be so large and monumental that *Infinite Intelligence* will give you an
overall sketch or outline. You are very likely to receive instructions in
the beginning telling you to complete XYZ. Then as you continue to
read your mission statement aloud, most usually within a few days or
a week, you will receive more instructions and directions. Your brain
will most likely help you realize and tell you, that in order to accomplish XYZ, you must first do MNO. (This is nothing more than your
subconscious giving you a list of objectives to complete in order to
reach your final goal. For our purpose, objectives can be classified as

measurable steps in accomplishing your goal.) Then a few more days pass and as you continue to read your mission statement out loud 2–3 times per day, you are liable to have another "aha" moment. This is when you say ok, in order to do MNO, I must first do ABC. In other words it will keep breaking it down, objective by objective, until you know exactly what to do on that exact ABC day, so you can set forth on attaining your Plane of Success. Some make a mistake at this point. Some think, now that I have my plan I no longer need to repeat my mission statement out loud. Do not be fooled by this. Here's why: there will be obstacles, or stumbling blocks along the way. Without having your mind's eye on the final prize and continuing to visualize yourself already being in possession or position, and reaching your Plane of Success, these obstacles can sidetrack you. You could be met with temporary defeat along the way, and without your subconscious mind pulling for you, and without you remaining steadfast in *faith*; you might have a tendency to give up. Another distraction that might come about (what appears to be a better opportunity), is usually contrary to what you have already established as your burning desire. Some who stop reading their mission statement will jump from one seemingly good opportunity to the next, never reaching their Plane of Success. This will not happen if you stay true to the instructions outlined in this book. Nothing can ever stop you, except yourself. You are in charge of your destiny, no one else.

Another example of expecting your subconscious or *Infinite Intelligence* to lay out for you a step by step plan the very first time you have an inspiration or flash, was described in the incredible book *Three Feet From Gold*, by Sharon L. Lechter and Greg S. Reid. Greg was interviewing Truett Carty, CEO of Chick-fil-A, when Mr. Carty gave him this advice, "Stop Planning so much." Right now, you are probably thinking the same thing that Greg thought. Stop planning so much goes against everything you've ever heard or been taught. Then Mr. Carty asked Greg a question. He asked, "You look like a pretty sharp fellow Greg. I'll bet you had a lot of plans this past year. How many of those plans actually worked out for you, step by step exactly as you had planned?" He then said, "Now, please understand that you may achieve some end result from time to time, meaning you hit a goal, but the way you intended to reach it probably differed from reality."

He then gave this excellent example: "Let's make it real simple. Let's say your goal is to get from one end of the street to the other. You start at one end and your goal is to reach the other. So you make a plan to put one foot in front of the other and possibly pause once in awhile for a rest, then continue with one foot in front of the other until you reach your goal." He continued, "Going about it this way, you might actually miss all of the unexpected opportunities." This confused Greg as he asked, "Opportunities?" Mr. Carty went on to explain that by him following his path of one foot in front of the other, then resting, then one foot in front of the other again, he might overlook the bicycle or skateboard setting there, that was available to ride to help make this journey quicker.

So here Greg spoke up again and said, "I totally get that. You have a destination in mind, move toward it, then seek opportunities to assist you along the way." Mr. Carty said, "Exactly, and if you're real lucky, a neighbor may drive by and let you hitch a ride, and you could be there in no time. It's okay to take huge steps in life; in fact to get ahead you might have to. It's also ok not to bet the farm on every decision you make. Give yourself a little breathing room."

Here is a good time to come to grips with this most beneficial tactic. In the Six Keys To Success you were instructed to not only write out your goal and the time limit for achievement, you were also instructed to read it and see yourself already in possession of reaching your Plane of Success. This is monumental in your practice. When you are visualizing already reaching your Plane of Success (with your eyes closed), see yourself taking the necessary lessons you will need to learn your art as well as visualize yourself practicing, without wavering, everyday until you accomplish your goal. Consider the old saying, "There are three ways to get to Carnegie Hall—Practice, Practice, Practice."

A note to ponder: Keep in mind while reading this book that much of this philosophy and these principles for success were shared and handed down through history from Mr. Andrew Carnegie (1835–1919), whose name is illuminated and celebrated at Carnegie Hall in New York City. It was his success in using these principles that profited the money and the gift to build such a magnificent stage. Can you see yourself playing there?

John Tesh, an acclaimed American pianist and composer of pop music said this: "The world is full of people who have dreams of playing Carnegie Hall, or running a marathon or owning their own business. The difference between the people who make it to that grand stage or finish line and everyone else, is one simple thing: A Plan of Action."

Have you written out your Plan of Action and what you plan to give in return for this?

Mick Jones, one of the founding members of Foreigner, a British-American rock band, had childhood dreams of playing Royal Albert Hall. He had seen a Gustav Holst (1874–1934) concert and was mesmerized as Sir Malcolm Sargent (1895–1967) conducted The Planets suite. Mick said, "One day, I will play from that stage," and decades later he fulfilled that dream.

Joe Diffie (1958–2020), American country music singer-songwriter, said, "As a little boy, I used to listen to the Grand Ol Opry on the radio and see myself playing there and belonging there." Years later on that famous stage, he made this statement,

"All of my other achievements pale in comparison and for the first time in my life I feel like I really belong to the country music family. I'm so overwhelmed with the emotion of that little boy's dream becoming reality. Thank you."

In reality he should have been thanking himself as it was his dream and he is the one who put in the time, effort and work to bring it about. Notice his use of the words, "see myself playing there." Can you visualize yourself reaching your Plane of Success?

100% Proven Formula to Reach Your Plane of Success

Here I will give you an exact example of the paragraph, I personally have been using since 1968. I have simply changed the dates and the exact goals throughout the years, however I have kept the same basic formula. I promise you, this will work for you. If you have *faith*, and you read aloud, add emotion into your words and visualize yourself already reaching your Plane of Success . . . you will arrive there.

First, I will share exact instructions on how and when to use this formula. I like to use 3x5 cards. In the early days, I used to laminate the card so it would not get so tattered. Then, the very first thing in the morning, I would read it out loud to myself. I usually read it in the bathroom where the rest of the family wouldn't think I had lost my mind. I also remember pulling my car over while driving to work. I would look at myself in the rear view mirror to read it extra loud with extra emotion, and extra conviction. I would also read it every time I went to the bathroom throughout the day. Sometimes given my situation, it did not permit me to read very loud due to other bathroom patrons. This repetition helps immensely in the memorization process. Again, it's important to read aloud in the beginning so you can be sure the vibrations are reaching your subconscious mind. Later you can repeat under your breath.

Then it is especially important to read at night. Find a quiet spot where you will not be disturbed or interrupted, and read it aloud, so you can hear your own words. Again, you are sending the vibrations of your voice and words so your subconscious mind will accept them and begin action to bring about your desire.

Once memorized, it is particularly important, as you drift off to sleep, to continue repeating and visualizing. This will put your dominating thoughts at the forefront of your mind leading directly to your subconscious. Then as you have already learned, your subconscious will continue to work on your goal all night long as you rest up for another exciting and productive day in the morrow.

I would like to try and make this as simple as possible, however there is one area that might seem contradictory. Let me explain.

When you first begin reading this book and digesting the information and instructions, it is specifically important to realize it is not necessary to know "how" you are going to reach your Plane of Success. What is of major significance is having the *faith* you will get there and visualizing yourself already there. In the beginning the "how" is the job you are sending to the subconscious for interpretation, suggestions and instructions.

If you are not 100% clear on what you have read regarding the "how to use" portion of the upcoming formula, go back and read again.

Example Paragraph

Let's suppose you intend to play violin for the New York Symphony Orchestra. Your very first sample paragraph might read something like this:

I _____, am going to play violin in the New York Symphony Orchestra by February 14, 20XX. I will do this by continuing my schooling, learning everything I need to know and meeting the people required to accomplish my goal. I know I have the ability to achieve this, therefore I demand of myself persistent and continuous **Action** toward its attainment and I shall never stop trying until I have accomplished my goal. I will let nothing stop me. My faith is so strong; I can see myself sitting in my chair, surrounded by the other players in the New York Symphony Orchestra. I am smiling and filled with pride and joy. I did it! I knew I could!

As I have said, while beginning this process, you do not need to know exactly how you will accomplish your goal. Keep in mind, your sentence that starts: I will do this by . . . will change from time to time to accommodate your progress and newly discovered insight, which will come to you through your subconscious and your sixth sense. By this point in time, I hope you're getting excited as you realize you can and will reach your Plane of Success.

It's important to write this out in your own handwriting. There is something magical about your brain recording it as it sees the words you are writing down.

When you originally imagined your goal to reach your Plane of Success, there might have been a time when you felt overwhelmed by the grandeur of your dream.

However, when you write out your goal and mission statement, most feelings of anxiety and feelings of being overwhelmed will usually subside. Keep in mind the fact that your major goal will be broken down into smaller objectives. This will once again strengthen your sense of self-confidence, and help you overcome the feeling of being mind-boggled.

The final step is to follow the "where and when and how" to read. At first these instructions might seem impractical or abstract. Do not let this unhinge you in any way. Follow these instructions to the letter. It is normal to be skeptical in the beginning. For one, you might not have yet developed the *faith* required to grasp the power of this new type of thought. Second, you might ask, if it's this easy why doesn't everybody practice this method?

I can tell you that over the years I have suggested Napoleon Hill's book, *Think and Grow Rich* to hundreds and hundreds. I have had a multitude of conversations with people who say, "Oh I read that book, it's a good book." However to make my point, most of those who I'm referring to, are found working mediocre jobs without much inspiration toward their future. Do you know what the difference is? Action. They did not take Action by writing out a mission statement and did not visualize themselves reaching a level of success higher than where they were. Or if they wrote out their mission statement, they quit reading it before their mind had developed the *faith* necessary to give themselves the persistence they needed. You can't expect to just read this mission statement then reach your Plane of Success. Possibly, they just read the book and agreed with the content, however took no action. You must take Action by writing out and committing to memory your goal, your desire, your dream, how you plan to get there and then seeing yourself already there. By seeing yourself already there, you are literally allowing yourself a "Mental Preview" of your final outcome in reaching your Plane of Success. Follow these instructions, to the letter.

Now I ask you, Do you like what you see?

THE PROFOUND PERCEPTION

Any dominating idea, plan or purpose held in the conscious mind through repetition of thought and emotionalized by a burning desire for its realization, is taken over by the subconscious and acted upon through whatever natural and logical means may be available.

When you take your *Burning Desire*, and mix it with *Faith*, then feed this paragraph, mission statement or mantra to your *Subconscious Mind* by using *Autosuggestion*, you have the formula for success.

The time will soon come when an entire new universe of power will unfold right before your eyes.

Will you be ready?

Chapter 3 QR Code Recap
Autosuggestion

Audio Only Duration 6:15 minutes

This QR Code excerpt was taken from the "Think and Grow Rich" Audio series Available at: www.nightingale.com

www.naphill.org/tgtam/chapter-3/

4
Specialized Knowledge

The Fourth Step Toward Reaching
Your Plane of Success

To begin with, I would like to bestow a profound selection of knowledge and understanding of music as Napoleon Hill expressed in one of his earliest essays, "The Effect of Music on Human Behavior."

"If the truth were known it might disclose the fact that music has been the strongest factor in producing the geniuses of the past. You do not have to go outside of your own experiences to prove that your most elevating thoughts come to you under the stimulating influence of music.

No man can say what part music has played and is not playing in unfolding and giving greater proportions to man's higher aspirations and in separating mankind from the basic animal instincts with which all of us are still too closely linked. No man can say that the musicians have not played a powerful part in bringing civilization up to its present standard.

Of all the people in the world who feel deeply, who pour their very heart and soul into their work, who are bound closely by that golden cord called sympathy for mankind, it seems that the musicians stand at the top of the list."

Now I ask you, isn't this music to your ears?

Are you from the school of thought that believes "Knowledge is Power?" I'm sure you've heard that statement before. Let me stop here and clarify Dr.Hill's philosophy. He states, "Knowledge is not power, knowledge is only potential power. It becomes power only when and if, it is organized into Definite Plans of Action and directed to a definite end."

He also states there are two kinds of knowledge; General Knowledge and Specialized Knowledge. Regardless of how you use general knowledge it is of little use in reaching your Plane of Success. You will never reach your Plane of Success unless the knowledge you possess is organized and intelligently directed through practical Plans of Action. Lack of understanding this fact has been the source of confusion to scores of people who believe knowledge is power.

Andrew Carnegie, who inspired this entire philosophy, genuinely believed in specialized knowledge. He believed that regardless of one's vocation or Definite Major Purpose in life, each person must eventually specialize. He suggested general education is advisable until you have selected your purpose in life. When you have found the right combination of your own desires, basic aptitudes and have the corresponding opportunity to utilize them, you should immediately begin to acquire specialized knowledge in your field of interest. In your case, this would be specialized knowledge in your medium of art, or your particular instrument and the style and genre you are pursuing. By remaining steadfast on your desire of reaching your Plane of Success, your mind will attract you to the specialized knowledge necessary.

You must learn how to organize and use knowledge after you acquire it. This is a crucial step. First the ability to acquire the necessary knowledge is needed, and then it is necessary to learn critical thinking skills so you can apply this knowledge. Knowledge without application is virtually useless in reaching your Plane of Success.

As I mentioned earlier, there are two types of knowledge . . . General and Specialized. On some level you will need specialized knowledge to reach your Plane of Success.

There are many ways to gain Specialized Knowledge. Libraries are stocked with helpful books and computers filled with information that might prove useful. There are also numerous periodicals and publications teeming with resourceful instruction regarding the area you seek in reaching your Plane of Success. There are specialized learning courses, night-school and correspondence classes, as well as universities teaching every form of art known to mankind. You can also gain knowledge from on-line platforms, chat and/or basic on-line schooling. With the onset of the Internet, access to education and practical information are available at the click of a button. Again, I want to caution you to be sure and verify any and all information you read on the Internet. Just because it's in print on your computer does not always make it true. You need to guarantee its accuracy before assuming it as factual.

I want to remind you that by merely gaining specialized knowledge does not guarantee you will reach your Plane of Success. All of the specialized knowledge in the world will not elevate you to that point unless you organize it and direct it through practical plans of action to a definite end.

Just because you are attending or have attended Juilliard in New York City, or Manhattan School of Music, the prestigious Berklee College of Music, The Oberlin Conservatory of Music, The Royal Academy of Music in London, The Conservatoire de Paris, Jacobs at Indiana University, The Shanghai Conservatory of Music, Curtis Institute of Music in Philadelphia, The University of Performing Arts in Vienna, The Los Angeles College of Music or any other higher learning platforms, does not guarantee you will reach your Plane of Success.

One final mention in my learning by repetition reminder; you must organize what you have learned and you must take **Action** toward reaching your Plane of Success. It can never be reached without **Action!**

While on the subject of schools I would like to share insight from one of the world's greatest violinists. I share this especially if you are pursuing a career in helping others by teaching. Mr. Itzhak Perlman stated: "I think music is one of the greatest, most inspired parts of an education. At least it should be. The problem lies with the teachers. Very rarely do you find a teacher so inspired with enthusiasm that it becomes infectious to the students. That's what we really need. I desire for others to feel the passion I feel toward music, however it's not easy in America, where society does not give much attention to music education."

Above, I mentioned several distinguished higher learning schools. I now pose the question, is it possible to reach your Plane of Success without attending such an institution? Yes, of course. Let's take a look at history.

Henry Ford (1863–1947), the auto magnate, had less than a sixth grade education, however you can see his name still driving on every major highway today.

Thomas Edison (1847–1931) had only three months of schooling in his entire life, and his many accomplishments are still marveled today as genius. How could we ever forget, he discovered the secret to recording sound back in 1877 by creating the first phonograph. Mr. Edison revealed to mankind during the first half of the twentieth century more of nature's secrets than had been previously uncovered in the entire history of civilization.

Chet Atkins (1924–2001), Grammy Lifetime Achievement Award Winner, songwriter, music producer and one of the most successful guitarists in history, never took a lesson. He created what became known as The Nashville Sound. Although he had influences, like all of us, he told me he never took a lesson or had proper schooling. I heard a younger player once ask him how he got so good without lessons, he replied, "First, I set a goal for myself to become famous playing the guitar. I then decided to devote my life to attaining my goal." I'm sure you have read about or are familiar with many great musicians who had but little training. Their training came by the way of Practice, Practice, Practice.

If you contemplate additional schooling, first determine the exact purpose for which you want and will use the knowledge you are seeking. Then do your homework by learning exactly where you can obtain this knowledge from a reliable source that has a good track record. Talk to others who have previously attended. Ask them, "If they had it to do over, would they go there again or somewhere else?"

Quincy Jones (American Record Producer, Actor, Conductor, Arranger, Composer, Musician, Television and Film Producer and Instrumentalist) said: "I used to practice piano for hours upon end, and now with a synthesizer, you can input the music and the machine perfects the song. This is one reason we have so many people in the music business who should have been plumbers. They really don't understand music because they weren't forced to practice to get it perfect or they haven't been trained." He continued, "All music has a soul, you just have to be true to it." In his humorous viewpoint he also stated, "You can't live without water or music."

What we do know for sure, regardless of the amount of specialized knowledge you acquire in the area of training . . . it's going to take a colossal amount of practice.

Using Knowledge and Goals to Overcome The Music Businesses Uncertainties

The music business can be quite fickle. It seems some gain success overnight. In any genre of music you will have the one-hit wonders;

Right place, right time, with the right beat to match. Another example could be getting picked up for a huge tour with a major artist. When the tour ends, you might be deflated with the feeling of no longer being on top. It's similar to the one-hit wonder scenario, where as they find themselves working back at a department store trying to make ends meet. There are also cases in which an entire audience has moved on, due to a new kid on the block.

This uncertainty surrounding the music business and these head-on challenges have brought many to the point of giving up. This is when you need to rekindle your belief and confidence in yourself.

Five Diva's Degrees of Determination

Mariah Carey (American Singer-Songwriter, referred to by The Guinness World Records as The Supreme Songbird—due to her 5 octave vocal range) said this about believing in yourself: "Who knows what miracles you can achieve when you believe in yourself." Some call the power of belief *magic*, Mariah refers to it as a miracle.

Carole King (American Composer, Singer-Songwriter, one of the most successful female songwriters of the latter half of the twentieth century) spoke of believing in yourself: "Do the things you believe in, in the name of love. Know that you aren't alone. We all have had doubts and fears. You must believe in yourself."

Aretha Franklin (1942–2018), American Singer-Songwriter . . . The Queen of Soul, put it bluntly: "Be your own artist, and always be confident in what you're doing. If you're not going to be confident, you might as well not be doing it. Never lose your confidence."

Mary J. Blige (American Singer-Songwriter, Record Producer, and Actress) said, "Continue to believe in yourself no matter how many times you fall down. Continue doing what you were born to do and don't ever give up. If I can do it, you can too."

Chaka Khan (American Recording Artist): "You've just got to follow your own path. You have to trust your heart and you have to listen
to the warnings . . . you can't argue with the universe. It's not about
that. It's more about relaxing and having the confidence in knowing
you can handle it and feeling empowered. Believing in yourself and
knowing you have the power to do whatever the hell you want to do.
That's what it's really about."

Do you find a common thread running through all five of these
declarations? Now we can safely say: "What the mind of man and
woman can conceive and believe, it can achieve."

As I have mentioned, the music business is and can be very tem-
peramental, changing directions with the wind. It is important for you
with your burning desire and unwavering courage to keep your long-
distant goals in front of you at all times. When you keep your mind on
your Plane of Success (long-term goal), it makes it easier to accept any
challenges or setbacks you might encounter in reaching your short-
term goals. In other words, when you have a target, it doesn't matter if
you need to make a detour to arrive there. You still have the same target, which makes it easier to overcome any obstacles. Again—by having a long-term goal, it makes the short-term failures easier to accept
and conquer.

There is little you can do to prevent changes in the music business. Labels change, radio formats change, management and manag-
ers come and go. However, what will not change is your desire and
your steadfast practicing that will keep you on the front lines toward
reaching and maintaining your Plane of Success.

Now that you have a set of goals to push you forward and help
maintain your focus, it's time to put them in order. Again, your short-
term goals are what lead you to your long-term goals. It is of major
importance to note the order in which to achieve these desires to
reach your Plane of Success.

Let's try an example of how your long-term might influence your short-term. Let's say for example, in reaching your Plane of Success your goal is to play bass guitar in a famous blues band. To do this you need a blues-band bass-playing skill set. Since all genres of music have their own styles, it would be essential for you to learn, practice and understand this unique style for you to ever be considered to play this part. To accomplish this you might need to establish some short-term goals. You might need to get lessons privately from someone with professional knowledge, who understands blues bass guitar and can lead you in the proper direction on how to study this exact art form and what you will need to know to move forward. One requirement would be to master a catalog full of blues standards and understand and play this style without missing a beat. You would also need to solo with perfection, a variety of blues oriented chord progressions. You must master the timing.

With this example you see the many moving parts associated with reaching your long-term goal and the many short-termers it takes to finally reach your Plane of Success. Once you get these in order, your entire world will become simpler and make more sense and become less overwhelming.

Beyoncé (American Singer-Songwriter, Actress, and Grammy winner) shared this in regards to setting goals. "I can never be safe. I always try and go against the grain. As soon as I accomplish one thing, I just set a higher goal. That's how I've gotten to where I am. I wanted to sell a million records, and I sold a million records. I wanted to go platinum and I went platinum. I have been working non-stop since I was fifteen. Your self-worth is determined by you! You do not have to depend on somebody telling you who you are. Do what you were born to do. You just have to trust in yourself. After all a true diva is graceful, talented, strong, fearless, brave, and maintains humility."

THE PROFOUND PERCEPTION

Any dominating idea, plan or purpose held in the conscious
mind through repetition of thought and emotionalized
by a burning desire for its realization, is taken over by
the subconscious and acted upon through whatever
natural and logical means may be available.

Chapter 4 QR Code Recap
Specialized Knowledge

Audio Only. Duration 9:33 minutes

This QR Code excerpt was taken from
the "Think and Grow Rich" Audio series
Available at: www.nightingale.com

www.naphill.org/tgtam/chapter-4/

5
Imagination

The Fifth Step Toward Reaching Your Plane of Success

The imagination is the workshop of the mind. Our minds are the greatest gift we possess. They visualize, compare, choose, analyze, foresee and provoke ideas. They tell us when to play, what to play and how to play. They tell us what to write, what to build, what to create and what to practice and for how long. When the imagination is forged with Napoleon Hill's famous quote; "Whatever the mind of man or woman can conceive and believe it can achieve"—there is no telling what can be accomplished! A wise man said, "Our job should be to imagine a better future, because if we can imagine it, then we can create it. It all starts with imagination." Without imagination nothing new would ever be created. Imagination is that activity of the mind that makes possible the creation of new ideas.

Have you ever had what you considered to be a good idea? Did your good idea bring you any closer to attaining your Plane of Success? If you said yes, then you are to be applauded. If not, let's jump in here and do as John Lennon (1940–1980) said, "Imagine."

You possess the most powerful idea factory in the world, it's on your shoulders. Your real boss is always the one who walks around under your hat. Your thoughts, ideas, insights and intuitions will manifest by using the creative power of your imagination. Imagination is the ability to create a mental picture of a thought, idea, insight or intuition in your mind. Your imagination is the most powerful tool in the world, because it can be used to create that which has never been seen. For any type of creative person, it's important for you to take that seed of talent that your Creator has given you and expand upon it by always looking for opportunities. At the end of the day, your task is to create something through your imagination that is of astounding beauty for all of mankind to enjoy. Continue to study and Practice, Practice, Practice. You must focus all your power on the end result you seek, in regards to realizing your Plane of Success. This is the only way to keep your ideas and your creative imagination from scattering. Form a mental picture. You must see yourself reaching your Plane of Success. This picture you visualize of yourself will act as your guide to keep you on track.

One of the greatest of all miracles is the power of creative thought. By using this power, you may translate the impulses of your thought into their physical, financial, or spiritual equivalents. This is the source of real power behind all achievement. It can bring either success or failure depending on how you use it.

Albert Einstein (1879–1955) stated, "Imagination is everything. It is a preview for life's coming attractions." Some of the most useful, innovative and influential creations have been developed from the simple act of someone simply imagining something easier, bigger, more eye appealing or less expensive. Some have imagined new ways to sell and distribute music: New players, new headphones, new formats and new, easier ways to teach music, which is exactly how tablature came about.

Can you imagine an entire new genre of music? Or imagine bringing an entire genre and style of music into the limelight such as what Bob Marley did with reggae, or what Buddy Holly, Elvis Presley, Chuck Berry, Bo Diddley, Little Richard and others did with rock and roll. Can you imagine yourself going way back in time to the era when Bach, Beethoven and Mozart were ushering in Classical Music? Then there was Woody Guthrie promoting folk music, Jimmie Rogers and Hank Williams, popularizing country music, Bob Wills rolling in the era of western swing. You can even reach back to Buddy Bolden creating his style of jazz, later popularized by Louis Armstrong, Joe King Oliver, Kid Ory and many others. Skrillex, David Guetta and Deadmau5 have emerged from the EDM (Electronic Dance Music) movement and achieved international popularity. Rap originators DJ Kool Herc, Coke La Rock and others, laid groundwork for an entire realm of hip-hop artists and rappers.

Within these genres there are many sub-genres that have emerged, too numerous to mention. If you open your mind to the possibilities of where these sub-genres emerged from, you will easily see most are merely offsprings from the main stream.

Is there a new offspring waiting for you to discover? It is important to think about the future, for after all, that is where we will be spending the rest of our lives.

Another example of creating something new, would be by examining the life of Martha Graham (1894–1991). Martha was an American modern dancer and choreographer. She created her style of dance commonly referred to as "The Graham Technique," which literally reshaped American Dance. Her techniques are still widely used today.

With regards and respect to all artists who paint or have painted, all have had a unique style that has been introduced possibly as a new spirit in art. Everything you paint is a new creation and the possibility of a new style. This creative vision comes to life through inspiration and the way you see things, which allows you to drink from its deepest wells. Leonardo Da Vinci sums it up with this quote, "Where the spirit does not work the hand, there is no art."

Scientists and creative artists have amazing skills and gifts when it comes to thinking outside the box, thus allowing their freedom to grow and evoke their thoughts. Many have created products that changed the way we live entirely. Imagination is one of the key ingredients to expansion and the advancement of our world. It does not matter whether this expansion is in the world of business, energy, any of the arts, entertainment or sciences—the advancement starts in the Imagination.

Follow Your Instinct

Justin Hayward (The Moody Blues) Rock and Roll Hall of Famer, ASCAP award winner of The Golden Note—a member of The Society of Distinguished Songwriters, and recipient of two Ivor Novello statues—the second award for "Outstanding Achievement," shared this advice with me. In regards to "following your dream," he said to "always trust your own judgment and your own instinct." Again it doesn't matter what "they" say. There will be those who try their best to discourage you and fill you with fear and doubt. Your job is to ignore them and use your own judgment to push forward. You don't have to attempt to be original or unique because you already are. Just be yourself and trust your own instinct.

Creative Instinct From Margaritaville

Jimmy Buffet (American singer-songwriter, actor and owner of the Margaritaville Brand) claims; instinct leads to creativity. He said "Humor has bailed me out of more tight situations than I can think of. If you follow your instincts and keep your humor by not taking yourself too seriously, creativity will follow. Always pay attention to older and wiser voices, they can help you find the right path, if you are only willing to listen." When asked about his challenges, he stated, "Quitting doesn't enter my mind."

Abilities Versus Disabilities

Itzhak Perlman (Israeli-American violinist, conductor, and music teacher; Grammy winner and recipient of the U.S. Medal of Liberty and National Medal of Arts) profoundly shared; "Separate your abilities from your disabilities." Stricken with polio at age 4, he did not let that stop him from following his dream of playing the violin. He said, "Everyday I would dream of becoming a master of the violin. I let my imagination govern my thoughts." He told himself, "I do not have to stand up to play. I will play sitting down." His greatest heroic tract is his determination to prevent his disability from interfering with his goals and dreams. He said, "Although I might have looked strange while playing, I did not give up on my dream of becoming a world class violinist. I dismissed all my doubts and did not focus on what I could not do, instead of what I could do, which was practice and play while sitting down."

Once while walking on crutches to his chair on stage, he fell. He did not ask for help. He wished to prove to others that being disabled was merely a title, it does not affect one's drive or ambitions in any way. His persistence has inspired many people who have ever felt and/ or feel like giving up on their musical dreams. He teaches that even through countless stumbles, everyone can be satisfied with themselves if they look at their mistakes with positive mindsets.

Conductor Perlman spreads hope and inspiration to disabled musicians ensuring them that nothing is impossible for a passionate heart. He shared that anyone can achieve his or her dreams if they have enough passion, enthusiasm and determination. He relates how difficult it is to overcome some obstacles in pursuing one's dream. His desire is to change the world for the better, by allowing more people to achieve happiness rather than give up early with belief of impossibility.

Two Forms of Imagination

Dr. Hill explains that our imagination facility functions in two forms. One is known as "Synthetic Imagination" and the other as "Creative Imagination."

Synthetic Imagination: "Through this faculty, one may arrange old concepts, ideas, or plans into new combinations. This faculty creates nothing. It merely works with the material experience, education, and observation of which it is fed. It is the faculty used most by the inventor with the exception of the 'genius' who draws upon the creative imagination, when he cannot solve his problem through synthetic imagination."

Creative Imagination: "Through the faculty of creative imagination, the finite mind of man has direct communication with *Infinite Intelligence*. This is the faculty through which 'hunches' and 'inspirations' are received. It is by this faculty that all basic, or new ideas are handed over to man. It is through this faculty that one individual may 'tune in' or 'communicate' with the subconscious minds of others."

The great leaders of business, industry, finance, and the great artists, musicians, poets and writers became great, because they developed the faculty of creative imagination. The imagination is just like a muscle. The more you exercise it, the stronger it becomes. I encourage you to read this entire book then come back to this chapter, and begin to put your imagination to work on building a plan to reach your Plane of Success. Reduce this plan to writing, if you have not already done so. By writing it down, you have given concrete form to your intangible desire.

I believe if you have read this far into this book, that you have a rather fertile imagination; one that sprouts seeds easily. Again muscles grow stronger through exercise. As stated before, the imagination is the workshop of the mind. You will need to spend sometime in your workshop, exercising.

The creative imagination works automatically. This faculty functions only when the conscious mind is working at an exceedingly rapid rate, such as when the conscious mind is stimulated through the emotion of a strong desire. Your creative faculty becomes more alert in direct proportion to its development through use, just as any muscle or organ in the body develops and becomes stronger by repeated use.

One way to exercise your imagination is by daydreaming. This is a very important tool to open your imagination and tap into your creativity. You remember when your teacher told you to "stop daydreaming?" Depending on the exact situation, that advice might have been less than desirable. When we daydream we take ourselves out of the ordinary moment and open ourselves up for exciting possibilities and ideas. These new ideas can bring about creativity, and isn't that what artists crave? So start daydreaming and enjoy those moments of creativity.

When you dare to dream and believe in your dreams you are the creator, of your future.

What do you want? Do you want to reach your Plane of Success by being a writer? Do you want to be a music or film producer? Do you want to be a professional photographer, sculptor, painter, potter, an anime, a glass artist, a performing artist of any type or an active player in any of the other arts? Do you want to be a major player? Do you want to work in the recording arena? Do you want to be a conductor? Then imagine it! How did The Creator create mankind? In "His Image." He created man in "His Image." He imagined man in His mind. What can you imagine?

It was Albert Einstein's imagination that led him to discover the theory of relativity, not his calculus and physics. He would see himself riding a beam of starlight up through space. Then when he just imagined what would happen if he were to sit astride this beam of starlight, he was then able to work out the mathematical formulas that proved his theory and help bring out his genius. It was his imagination.

Few ever use their imagination to its fullest potential. To be politically correct in today's world and social climate, we have been told that we are not acting like adults if we continue to stargaze, have pipe dreams and fantasize. This is why so many give up on their dreams. We let someone else's values affect our own lives and what we want. However, in this field of art and music, we are somewhat lucky in the fact that creative dreaming and the use of the imagination is still alive. Asking questions like, "What if," and "Do you think," are still accepted and can help trigger curiosity in your imagination.

Willie Nelson (Texas-born Singer-Songwriter, Author, Poet, Actor, and Activist) shared his insight: "If you wait 'til tomorrow to follow your dreams, it might be too late. By the time you get there, they might be gone." You need to take immediate action!

Dolly Parton (Singer, Songwriter, Actress, and Cultural Icon) gave this testimony regarding dreams: "That's what this whole dream world thing is about. You've got to dream it, then you've got to get out and work it and sometimes a dream can change right in the middle of it. You might really wind up with the ultimate dream. That's why you've got to keep dreaming . . . you never know what's going to happen."

Creativity is nearly a magical word. If you think you do not have creative skills like some others . . . think again. Every single time you have a new thought, it is a creation. Every time you dream up a new password your creative ability is displayed. Every new action, every new habit are your creations. No matter what you are doing in your life today or the time you spend putting your own natural spin on your life or activity . . . you are in your own unique way using one of your greatest gifts . . . your God-given creative power. It is only through these creative thoughts and actions that you bring to the surface your deep rooted hidden talents that often lie dormant within you. Your creative imagination is your ability to bring positive change and improvement into your life to help you reach your Plane of Success. Therefore embrace it, do not seesaw or shy away from your creativity. To understand your true capacity in reaching your Plane of Success you will need to learn to mix together your efforts with imagination. Can you imagine writing a number one song? Can you imagine conducting a modern day symphony? Can you imagine producing the record of the year? Can you imagine yourself painting a masterpiece that hangs in MOMA?

The Mirror Of Your Mind

Let's take a little more in-depth look. Let's look at your vision. First, are you able to see yourself already reaching your Plane of Success? Just close your eyes and see yourself already there. Now take your vision a step further. Is your painting being touted as one of the greatest of all times? Imagine it is. Or is the symphony you are conducting or orchestrating a symphony written by you? Imagine it is. Does everyone smile with excitement when your number one song is played? Imagine so. Just as I asked the above questions, it is also most important for you to ask yourself questions. Instead of saying, "I can't," say "How can I?" When you say, "I can't," you are closing your mind, however when you say, "How can I?" it opens your mind and triggers creativity. Let's revisit the path of some of these great scientists, inventors, and artistic people in general. Where did they get their ideas, dreams and visions? How is it possible for a composer to hear an entire symphony in his mind as if he had been practicing it for years, when in reality it is entirely new to him?

The Man In The Mirror King of Pop's Vision

When Michael Jackson (1958–2009) sought to reshape and transform his image from being the front man for The Jackson Five and later The Jacksons, he wrote this following note. It's somewhat of a mission statement.

> MJ will be my new name. No more Michael Jackson. I want a whole new character, a whole new look. I should be a totally different person (sic). People should never think of me as a kid who sang "ABC," and "I Want You Back." I should be a new, incredible actor/singer that will shock the world. I will do no interviews. I will be magic. I will be a perfectionist, a researcher, a trainer, a masterer (sic). I will be better than every great actor roped into one. I "must" have the most incredible training system. To dig and dig and dig until I find. I will study and look back on the whole world of Entertainment and perfect it. Take it steps further from where the great left off.

This was a handwritten note that he wrote to himself. It was read in Spike Lee's documentary, *Michael Jacksons' Journey from Motown to Off The Wall*. There is also one more line of great interest. He wrote, "I want to be the greatest entertainer of all time."

It's true we can't all be, or even want to be Michael Jackson or for that matter the "greatest entertainer of all time." However, you can take from his vision, to gain confidence in yours.

THE PROFOUND PERCEPTION

Any dominating idea, plan or purpose held in the conscious
mind through repetition of thought and emotionalized
by a burning desire for its realization, is taken over by
the subconscious and acted upon through whatever
natural and logical means may be available.

If not put here on earth by Our Creator, then all that exists first originated in the form of an idea. Ideas are resources that have no fixed values. In all parts of the world, people of all ages have identified the monumental importance of ideas. There is a famous old Asian proverb that goes like this:

If you plant for days—plant flowers;
If you plant for years—plant trees;
If you plant for eternity—plant *Ideas!*

Alvin Lee (1944–2013) of the blues-rock band Ten Years After spoke of his viewpoint on creativity. After he had written one of their top forty hits, he stated:

"When I wrote 'I'd Love To Change the World,' it came from the ether, *Infinite Intelligence*. It's like I just reached up and grabbed it from somewhere. Then I asked myself, where did that song come from?"

Willie Nelson put it this way; "I have so many songs that fall from the sky, all I can do is catch them before they hit the ground."

There is a lesson that history teaches: Repetition! Constant repetition carries conviction. Once again I impress upon you, by repetition, the examples that seemingly gifted artists have shared time and time again regarding their creativity.

Leonard Cohen in regards to his songwriting said: "If I knew where good songs come from, I'd go there more often! They seem to float in the air until they make their way into my brain."

Sir Paul McCartney (English Singer Songwriter who gained world wide fame as bass player and multi-instrumentalist for The Beatles) made a general statement relating to the overall view of creativity. "I think people who create art and write music, it actually does flow—just flows into their heads from above, then into their hands and to their pen where they write it down."

Do you, my loyal *Think and Grow Through Art and Music* reader, ever get the idea that all these tunesmiths are drawing from the same pool of knowledge? How could they unknowingly tap into this universal warehouse? Could it be that their enthusiasm, confidence, desire, imagination and emotion combined, has sped up their vibrations of thought, thereby uniting with *Infinite Intelligence*?

What Are the Characteristics of Infinite Intelligence?

I would like to now share with you the 12 characteristics of *Infinite Intelligence* as written by Dennis Kimbro in his praiseworthy book, *Think and Grow Rich—A Black Choice.*

I share them and his following thoughts because of their great significance relating to your required need in the use of creativity in reaching your Plane of Success.

Infinite Intelligence is likened to the creative power, which directs and governs the universe. This power has commonly been referred to as *The Universal Mind*, *The Great Unseen*, *The Divine Mind*, and *The Ether*. In addition,

1. It is the source of all pure creativity. Innovation is invariably the result of *Infinite Intelligence*.
2. It is the source of all inspiration. Whenever you feel inspired or uplifted, chances are that *Infinite Intelligence* has been activated within you. It is the source of all intuition—the voice of *Infinite Intelligence* is the intuitive voice. It is the source of all hunches or gut feelings.
3. It functions daily in conjunction with our subconscious. Even as you sleep, *Infinite Intelligence* remains steadfast, activating new ideas, vision, and dreams.
4. It works best with clear, specific goals. The more clear and more specific the goal; the more rapidly *Infinite Intelligence* can develop the ideas you require.
5. It automatically and continuously solves every problem as you move toward your goal—as long as the goal is defined! This is the reason why people who start life from humble beginnings can arrive at positions of prominence and influence.
6. It grows in power as it is used and believed in.
7. It gives you the lessons you need in order to be successful. It is through *Infinite Intelligence* that you will obtain wisdom and insight.
8. It operates best with an attitude of confident expectation. This is the psychic fuel that feeds this principle.
9. It brings you the answer you require at the right time. The answers to your problems will always come when you need them the most. But a word of caution—when you receive your answers, you must take Action immediately. Lost ideas may be difficult to recover. Write them down whenever they occur.

10. It makes all your words and actions, fit a pattern consistent with your dominant goals. When you've tapped into this life force, you will find yourself saying the right words, to the right people, at the right time.

11. It responds to emotionalized commands—affirmations—whether they are positive or negative.

12. It brings into reality any thought, goal, plan, or idea held within your conscious mind. *Infinite Intelligence* is capable of goal-oriented motivation and will release ideas for goal attainment and reaching your Plane of Success.

You will never know what your capacity for achievement is until you learn to mix your efforts with imagination. The products of your hands, *minus imagination*, will yield you but a small return. Those same hands, when properly guided by imagination, can take you directly up the path to reach your Plane of Success.

Being creative could prove to be your greatest asset. How creative can you be? How many ways can you be creative? How many great ideas or how many "aha" moments might you claim if you were to devote a few minutes each day to creative thinking? When you truly discover, that success in all areas of life have their starts by simply employing the creative process that lies within, you then become one giant step closer in reaching your Plane of Success. Research proves that your ability to tap into this deeper area of the mind, and having *faith* in your subconscious mind, then mixed with *Infinite Intelligence*, will determine your level of success. In the process of reaching your Plane of Success you are going to need both hands. One hand will be stretched upward to receive the many blessings of *Infinite Intelligence*. The other will be extended outward to share and give to others the gifts you have received. No one ever achieves outstanding success without the cooperation of others.

Igniting Your Creative Spark

In his creative and resourceful book, *Creative Quest*, Questlove (Four time Grammy winner, DJ, music producer, film and television producer, culinary entrepreneur, author and co-founder of The Roots), shares insight regarding creativity by what he refers to as "the departure." He states: "Creative people have specialties but also restlessness." He explores how to keep on doing the things you're doing, while also doing other things. He explores how to keep your talent sharp, while still looking for ways to "expand your talent."

Questlove goes on to say, "The only way your life will stay the same, in terms of creative inspiration and creative energy, is to make an effort to make your life 'different.' Meditation helps you switch the channel when it comes to what is moving through you. This meditative departure helps you switch the channel when it comes to how you are moving through the world.

"If you're a musician, don't forget to look at paintings. If you're a songwriter, read about subjects that are unfamiliar to you. If you are a singer, draw cartoons. If you are a writer, try to sculpt. Creative people have some impulse inside of them that compels them to approach material. That material may vary. But when you approach it, you approach it with a certain attitude. It's an attitude of change. If you have one of these creative attitudes, then you are a creative person. If you are a creative person, then the things you make by definition are creative. These departures will inform you. They will enlarge you. They will shape your sensibility, or reshape it. They will nourish you in moments when you might otherwise feel as though you're starving, creatively speaking."

All of Questlove's suggestions and insights are assimilated from his three plus decades of artistic creation. They are designed to help you ignite that creative spark that lies inside of you. His recommendations could prove to be of great benefit, especially if you find your-self plagued by writer's block or general lack of creativity. By his term "departure" . . . or shifting gears momentarily, you can possibly bring a new breath of life into your artistic avenue.

Napoleon Hill makes another profound observation, regarding Infinite Intelligence, "From the Time of Socrates (470 B.C.–399 B.C.), the founder of *ethical science*, to the inventive Thomas Edison, Henry Ford, and George Washington Carver (1864–1943), this little—under-stood area of mental activity, has delivered the insight and know-how for almost every great achievement that makes possible and sustains modern civilization as we know it."

If you will now take your **Desire**, or better yet, your **Burning Desire**, add in your newly found unwavering *Faith*, guided by your own set of personal **Autosuggestion** instructions, apply the **Specialized Knowledge** you have received and then decisively and by design sprinkle your **Imagination** upon it . . . you are well on your way to understanding this philosophy which will eventually deliver you to your desired Plane of Success.

Chapter 5 QR Code Recap
Imagination   Audio Only Duration 2:33 minutes

This QR Code excerpt was taken
from the "Think and Grow Rich"
Audio series
Available at: www.nightingale.com

www.naphill.org/tgtam/chapter-5/

6
Organized Planning

The Sixth Step Toward Reaching
Your Plane of Success

The Crystallization of Desire Into Action

What do you want to achieve or avoid? The answers to this question are objectives. How will you go about achieving your desired results? The answer to this is called "strategy."
— WILLIAM E. ROTHSCHILD, 1933 G.E. EXECUTIVE

Quincy Jones: "There's nothing in the world worse than having an opportunity that you're not prepared for. This sometimes can become the biggest mistake you've ever made. I see it all the time. I also see how 'Good luck' usually follows the collision of opportunity and preparation. 'Good luck' is a result of that collision. You've got to be prepared. You must plan for it. So make your mistakes now and make them quickly. You make your mistakes to learn how to get to the good stuff. Once you've made the mistakes you know what to do next time. This is how you become valuable to those around you. Plan with a purpose."

Here is where we figure out together how to "work your plan and plan your work." Judith Williamson, retired director of Napoleon Hill World Learning Center, oversees the extensive library of Dr. Hill's work. Here she shares her strategy for Organized Planning and provides practical advice for us to utilize.

The Payoff in Organized Planning

Organized Planning is essential to everyone's success. From writing a book, to constructing a dollhouse, to preparing a dinner, they all demand advance planning and preparation. The same is true in building a successful career or business. An organized, and detailed plan is critically important for charting your course to success.

Once my overall plan is set, I construct a daily-to-do list of ten or more essential items I want to accomplish that day, that will help me reach my long-term goals. The simple task of crossing it off the list makes me feel great that I have accomplished something. I challenge myself to start with the least appetizing item on the list, as accomplishing it will jump-start my day.

Since we all multitask, it is important to address issues related to our spiritual, physical, mental, social, emotional, creative and financial goals, so that we care for our whole being. If not, you could find yourself successful financially, but not healthy enough to enjoy it.

By beginning your itemized list with verbs such as 1) *wash* the car, 2) *clean* the bathroom, and 3) *write* the chapter; it will help you be motivated to take the action listed, and it will be easy to discern at the end of the day whether you accomplished your goal.

As you accomplish smaller objectives that contribute to larger goals, inch-by-inch, step-by-step and yard-by-yard, the process begins to take on a new life of its own.

As an example, when noticing things around the house, aren't you ever astonished as to how quickly things accumulate? Newspapers that arrive daily stack up to create a heavy load by the end of the week. Mail scattered on the dining room table soon covers the tabletop horizontally and begins to stack up vertically if left unsorted.

Refrigerators filled with leftovers for "later" literally soon begin to take on a life of their own. These are just mundane examples of how the tendency is for things to accumulate. By creating a to-do list and focusing on your intention to declutter for a reasonable period each day, you will find that you have achieved a great deal by the end of the month. This cosmic pattern can be replicated for all our desirable goals and objectives once we understand how to put this natural law to our best use.

I perform best when I am organized. A former boss used to tell me that a folder for each project I was working on, would be all the organization I needed to succeed. When I navigated from one project to the next, I would place whatever notes, receipts, memos, etc., I had accumulated into the folder. I also kept a printout of my calendar with related appointments and phone calls to help jog my memory later. The folder is always waiting for me the next time I need it. It's a simple system that works, if you use it.

Organized planning is crucial to anyone's success. But even the most organized individual needs to have a pleasing personality, creating friendly and authentic human relationships. Also needed is trust, sincerity, and genuine common interest in everyone's betterment. By intentionally following the golden rule of "do unto others as you would have others do unto you," we can begin the process of making the world better—starting with bettering ourselves.

The only person we can truly change lives inside of us. Fundamentally the truth is, that change begins with us, and when we change, everything around us changes.

Now that you have read Judy's suggestions and benefits of organized planning, it's time to see how this fits into your daily routine.

As I previously mentioned, by using Autosuggestion to feed your subconscious and conscious mind you will suddenly start flowing with ideas and instructions. It's important to write these down as soon as they appear. You are being guided to take certain steps so you can eventually reach the top of the staircase. Usually these steps will need to be broken down even further to baby steps. This is where Judy's numbering system comes into complete understanding and practicality.

As you set about to reach your Plane of Success you will have many other daily requirements and necessities to accomplish. Depending upon your burning desire and the *faith* you have in yourself to accomplish this desire . . . there will be days when your list of to-do's will be off the page. Beginning at once and completing a given task on your to-do list, is in reality where the action begins and your dreams come one step closer to reality.

Years ago, I learned a practice which has been most beneficial to me. First, write a list of everything you can think of that you need to accomplish in the days ahead. Then take a serious look at all of the items on your list. Randomly put a number next to them by order of importance. Number them 1–10. Then take **Action** to complete number one and then move on to number two, etc. Sometimes by crossing off a number it would also create more tasks, phone calls or emails for later or for the following day, which need to be noted.

The following day you can either start on the next uncompleted number or I sometimes find it much easier and more organized to start a new list . . . again numbering 1–10 by order of importance. I like Judy's self-starting commands with her use of verbs, such as call, clean, go to, etc.

Another tip that might prove useful concerns the tasks you keep moving from list to list without seeming to complete. After a few days, reevaluate the task and ask yourself, why you have not completed it as of yet. By concentrating on this challenge you will usually find out why. Then make it number one for the following day, and without thinking about it, get up, and as Nike says, "Just do it." Sometimes we have a tendency to put so much thought and anticipation into a task that we talk ourselves out of it before even starting. "Just do it!" You will feel better, it will boost your level of confidence and who knows, it might elevate you a few steps closer to grasping your Plane of Success.

Incidentally, I consistently used the same type of steno pad for this activity. If I still had all the steno pads I had used in the past, they would probably stack up to several floors high. By using the exact, or nearly exact, type of notepad consistently year in and year out, it will help you with staying focused and organized. Merely seeing it throughout the day might spur you into **Action**.

Action itself is essential in reaching your Plane of Success. You can possess a desire, you can have all the specialized knowledge in the world, however without action you are at a standstill. W. Clement Stone (1902–2002), claimed to be the first multi-millionaire, by using Napoleon Hill's philosophy for success. In Hill's later years, Mr. Stone was also Napoleon's General Manager. Here he shares his own personal, self-starter, to springboard one's self into **Action**. He made it very simple for us. When you are having a challenge getting started with any task, no matter how big or small, he suggests saying three words approximately ten times or however many times it takes you to spring into **Action**. What are the three magic words? **"DO IT NOW."** I had great success by adding one more technique to this practice. While saying Mr. Stone's, three self-starting words, over and over, visualize yourself starting, performing and completing the task. Notice your smile of confidence when you see yourself completing this less than desirable, however obviously necessary task. Personally, I have probably said these words **"DO IT NOW,"** thousands upon thousands of times in my lifetime. Try it. Say, **"DO IT NOW," "DO IT NOW," "DO IT NOW,"** and visualize the all-encompassing joy you will feel by starting to finalize whatever particular undertaking you are trying to achieve.

Now that you understand just how important it is to take Action, you must also take a look at the importance of your strategy. No matter how sincere, passionate, honest and stately your intentions might be, and the action you take, without a strategy they could prove to be fruitless.

According to the Business Dictionary, Strategy is defined as: *A method or plan chosen to bring about a desired future, such as achievement of a goal or solution to a problem.*

Once again, we are back to planning our work and working our plan. Alan Lakein, a time management expert said, "Failing to plan is planning to fail." Do you yet have a plan? As you learned earlier you don't necessarily want or need an exact step-by-step plan because this will change as you progress. You do however, always need the end goal in sight. The steps of getting there might vary and change . . . usually for the better.

Formulating a plan, and a strategy is a must as you are on the road to reaching your Plane of Success. The vast majority of people get up every morning with the plan of doing exactly what they did the day before. Most seem unsure and have not a slightest clue of which direction they are headed. As the old adage states—they are like a ship without a rudder—heading any way the wind blows. Due to the fact they are operating without a plan or strategy, they are heading down the long and winding road of indecisiveness and uncertainty. So often they have more than enough talents to become a success, however they have no direction, no strategy or course of beneficial **Action**.

Astronaut Jim Lovell said, "There are three types of people. One—those who take action and make things happen; Two—those who stand and watch things happen; and Three—those who sit and wonder what happened." By taking action, as a reader of *Think and Grow Through Art and Music* you will remain number one and make things happen.

Les Paul said, "I have always followed my plan and my impulses to carry forward to the next thing that drove my curiosity. This helped me get the most out of the gifts I was born with. The difference between just thinking and actually doing, and taking Action is what set me apart from others more than anything else. I always said, somebody has to do it and that somebody is me."

Although he was a constant joker, I believe Les Paul shared more thoughtful insight and had a true understanding of why and what I am trying to help you accomplish by studying *Think and Grow Through Art and Music*.

Short Termers

Once you have your Plane of Success lined out with your final goal in mind, your subconscious will automatically break down exactly what needs to be done. When the instructions come, and they will, as I have previously instructed, write them down immediately. This is when and how you establish your short-term goals . . . one step at a time.

For example, if your Plane of Success requires special schooling, this will take money. If you are to earn this yourself, you need to know the amount of money and the date you need it by, in order to pay for your schooling.

Once you know the amount required and the date you need it by, you should begin at once. You first need to write out your short-term mission statement. Your mission statement should include the amount of money required and the date you would need it by. The date you need it by, would be determined by the timing of when the next class starts, as well as a date you think you can realistically begin. Don't forget to add emotion when submitting this goal to your subconscious. You might not have an idea where the extra money will come from, just believe you will have it and your subconscious will do the rest. Equally as important, is to see yourself already in possession of this money. Picture yourself holding it in your hand or picture a mental photo of your bank account with your name at the top, depicting a balance of X amount of dollars you require. This same short-term mission statement process will apply to any and all necessities that stand between you and the road leading to your Plane of Success.

If your Plane of Success requires a special instrument or instruments or technical supplies of any nature, then you need a clear picture of the exact instrument(s) and or supplies and the cost. Again your short-term mission statement can help you acquire what you need. These are examples of short-term goals that can be reached quite quickly. Here it becomes a matter of managing your time and your energy. As I mentioned, you do not need to know how or where you will get what you need, you only have to see and believe you will have what's needed and the method of getting it, will come to you. Depending on your exact situation, you might need a second job or with schooling, you might look for financial assistance.

Accomplishing short-term goals such as these will give you confidence in this philosophy and allow you to always push on with forward momentum. So now we find ourselves back at the staircase landing. It would be nice to take one giant leap and reach the top immediately. In reality it does not work that way. You must start exactly where you are and take one step at a time by setting these short-term goals. By taking one step at a time you will eventually reach the top. When you arrive, you will look back down and realize the amount of steadfast work you have put forth, which in turn helps you realize not only how worthy you are, but how anything of worthwhile value takes dedication, planning, strategy, action and hard work.

Are You A Leader?

Do you want to be the leader of your band? Do you want to conduct an orchestra? Do you want to be an art teacher? Do you want to lead yourself by being a solo act? Do you want to lead students in any of the arts?

It doesn't matter what your Plane of Success might be, in one way or another you are going to be a leader even if it's no more than leading yourself.

I would be remiss not to mention the eleven attributes of leadership as outlined here by Napoleon Hill. You will need to master each one of these to become a successful leader.

1. Unwavering Courage
You must display self-confidence and courage.

2. Self-Control
You must be able to control yourself in all areas of life, especially substances.

3. A Keen Sense of Justice
You must be fair to retain the respect of your followers or those you are leading.

4. Definiteness of Purpose

You must not waver in your decisions; you must show that you are sure of yourself.

5. Definiteness of Plans

You must display you have an exact plan and stick to it regardless of circumstances.

6. The Habit of Doing More Than Paid For

You must display the willingness to go the extra mile and do more than those you are leading. (A guaranteed method of getting a raise or promotion on your day job.)

7. A Pleasing Personality

This is most important no matter what you are trying to achieve; a necessity, beneficial in every walk of life. I suggest reading Dale Carnegie's excellent work from 1936, *How To Win Friends and Influence People* or even consider taking his course, which is available in nearly every major city.

8. Sympathy & Understanding

You must be in sympathy with your followers and understand their problems.

9. Master of Detail

Successful leadership calls for mastery of details of the leaders position.

10. Willingness to Assume Full Responsibility

As a leader you must assume full responsibility for all mistakes and shortcomings of those you are leading. You cannot shift the blame elsewhere. You must always consider their failure as your failure.

11. Cooperation

As a successful leader, you must understand and apply the principle of cooperative effort and induce your followers to do the same. Leadership calls for power and power calls for cooperation.

Napoleon goes on to make this statement: There are two forms of leadership, the first, and by far the most effective, is leadership by consent. Here is when you have the full cooperation and the sympathy of your followers. (Again I interject and suggest you read *How To Win Friends and Influence People*). The second is leadership by force, or without the consent and sympathy of your followers.

History is filled with examples of how leadership by force has failed and cannot endure. The downfall and disappearance of dictators and kings should be significant proof that people will not follow forced leadership indefinitely. Leadership by consent is the only brand that will endure. Leadership by consent is where you suggest and they willingly follow so you all reach the same goal.

He also states that it is just as essential to know and understand what *Not To Do* as it is *What To Do*, he now gives us The Ten Major Causes of Failure in Leadership.

The Ten Major Causes of Failure In Leadership

1. **Inability to organize details.** Efficient leadership calls for ability to organize and to master details. You can never be "too busy" to do anything which may be required of you in your capacity as leader. When you admit that you are "too busy" to change your plans, or to give attention to any emergency, you admit your inefficiency. You must be the master of all details connected with your position. That means, of course, that you must acquire the habit of delegating responsibilities.

2. Unwillingness to render humble service. You must be willing, when occasion demands, to perform any sort of labor, in which you might ask another to perform.

3. Expecting to be paid for what you know, rather than what you do with what you know. The world will not pay you for what you know. It will pay you for what you do, or induce others to do.

4. Fear of competition from followers. If you fear one of your followers may take your position you are practically sure to realize that fear sooner or later. You may, through your knowledge and the magnetism of your personality, greatly increase the efficiency of others.

5. Lack of imagination. Without imagination, you are incapable of meeting emergencies, and of creating plans by which to guide your followers efficiently.

6. Selfishness. If you claim all the honor for the work of your followers, it is sure to be met by resentment. The really great leader claims none of the honors.

7. Intemperance. Followers do not respect an intemperate leader. Moreover, intemperance in any of its various forms destroys the endurance and the vitality of all who indulge in it.

8. Disloyalty. Perhaps this should have come at the head of the list. If you are not loyal to your trust, and to your associates, those above you and those below you will not respect your leadership. Lack of loyalty is one of the major causes of failure in every walk of life.

9. **Emphasis of the "authority" of leadership.** You must lead by encouraging, and not by trying to instill fear in the hearts of your followers. If you are a real leader, you will have no need to advertise that fact. Your conduct—your sympathy, understanding, fairness, is a demonstration that you are a leader.

10. **Emphasis of title.** You require no "title" to get the respect of your followers.

These are among the most common of the causes of failure in leadership. Any of these faults is sufficient to induce failure. Study the list carefully. You want to be free of these faults regardless of who you are leading.

Now that you realize what you must do, and not do, to become an effective leader, you must also take a look at the decision process. The next chapter on Decision, will not only guide you in becoming a more efficient leader, it will also speed up your progress in reaching your Plane of Success. In closing this chapter, I leave you with;

THE PROFOUND PERCEPTION

Any dominating idea, plan or purpose held in the conscious
mind through repetition of thought and emotionalized
by a burning desire for its realization, is taken over by
the subconscious and acted upon through whatever
natural and logical means may be available.

Chapter 6 QR Code Recap

Organized Planning   Audio Only Duration 4:19 minutes

This QR Code excerpt was taken from

the "Think and Grow Rich" Audio series

Available at: www.nightingale.com

www.naphill.org/tgtam/chapter-6/

7
Decision

The Seventh Step Toward Reaching Your Plane of Success

Procrastination is the opposite of decision. It is a common enemy, which practically every man and woman must conquer.

How many times have you said, "Oh, I'll do that when I get some extra time." Or, "I keep meaning to do such and such but just haven't got around to it yet." Have you ever waited until the very last minute to complete a project, causing yourself unneeded stress and possibly not giving yourself the proper amount of time required to complete the task properly? Procrastination breeds indecision and indecision breeds procrastination. Stop procrastinating and become a doer. Doers see accomplishments. There is a common trait that runs through successful people in all fields of endeavor.

Every successful person has the habit of **Reaching Decisions Promptly** and **Changing These Decisions Slowly**, if and when they are changed. Likewise, Dr. Hill pointed out, *"People who fail, without exception have the habit of reaching decisions, if at all, very slowly, and of changing these decisions quickly and often."*

By combining your **Burning Desire** with your **Definite Major Purpose** and using **Autosuggestion** to convince yourself that you will attain your **Plane of Success**, it makes it easier to reach major decisions quicker and with more determination and self-assuredness.

Most artists and musicians who fail are those who are easily influenced by others. They take what others say to heart. They will let their friends, family members and associates influence their thinking and their beliefs. They hear certain words that stick in their psyche such as, "You'll never make it, you're not good enough, you are a dreamer or even, you don't look right."

Thousands of men and women carry inferiority complexes with them all through life, because some well-meaning, but ignorant person destroyed their confidence through "opinions" or "ridicule."

In Dr. Hill's book, *Outwitting The Devil*, which was brilliantly edited and annotated by Sharon Lechter, the Author of *Think and Grow Rich for Women*, the concept of "drifting" was introduced. He states; "A drifter is someone who permits himself to be influenced and controlled by circumstances outside his own mind . . . one who accepts what life throws his way without making a protest or putting up a fight." It is the drifters who are easily dominated by the opinions of others, and find themselves derailed at every turn. He said, non drifters, were driven by their "Definiteness of Purpose," and their "Burning Desire." Due to their goals they could not be swayed.

The habit of indecision typically begins during your youth and can only be counteracted by finding your "Definiteness of Purpose" and the "Desire" to succeed.

You must remember that your world will change whether or not you choose to change it. You have the power to choose its direction. You can set your own path toward reaching your Plane of Success. You have your own desires and ambitions. You have your own brain and mind. Use their assets to reach your own decisions. When you need to gather facts or information from other people, it's best sometimes to do so without disclosing your purpose. It is human nature for someone to feed you negative information to keep you from attaining your goals. Others think because "they" can't do something, that you can't either. They think to themselves, if I can't do it with all my knowledge, then how could he or she ever hope to. It sometimes is their envy, which makes them want to cast doubt and fear into your desires. Therefore, they input their negative viewpoints, which in turn can impact your way of thinking as well. You must put up your guard and once again do not listen to what "they say." Practice pulling the curtains shut on all negativity, always. They do not know or understand you possess the magic secret, and the formula to reach your Plane of Success.

Eric Clapton (English guitarist, Singer-Songwriter and three time Inductee into the Rock and Roll Hall of Fame) said, "One of the most beneficial things I've learned in becoming a musician is to keep my mouth shut."

As you devour your music and art instructions, guidance, schooling and all realms of learning, keeping your mouth closed and your ears open, will give you the opportunity to gain more knowledge. Likewise your eagerness and your desire to learn will impress upon your master, teacher or professor, which will trigger more effort from them to make sure you understand the material. This goes back to some basic roots and philosophy for dealing with people in general. By showing a keen interest and having your ears open to what is being taught, and by asking questions, you in essence are giving your instructor a feeling of importance.

I could write an entire chapter on this subject, however for our purpose today, I want you to comprehend fully the realization that everyone likes to feel important in one way or another. By giving undivided attention to your instructor and asking questions and demonstrating that you are grasping their concepts, then in reality you are praising them with a feeling of importance. When they feel important, they automatically feel better about themselves, and they are going to bask in that self-importance. In turn, as an instructor they will help you learn on a deeper level, than if you merely just show up for class. It's important to remember that most people will work harder for a word of praise than any other form of payment. The desire for recognition is one of the Ten Basic motives that inspires voluntary action.

Tell and Show

One of the first decisions you must make is to keep a governor on your mouth and keep your eyes and ears open at all times. Remember the old adage or epigram "Tell the world what you intend to do, but first show it."

Only talk about your Definite Major Purpose and your plan to succeed with those who are, or those who will be, in your Master Mind alliance. By talking about your purpose and your goals to those who have little interest, you in essence, are losing your power. People who are jealous, and not in sympathy with your plan of success, will use your loose tongue as ammunition to defeat or ridicule you. You do not need this negative input. Some people like nothing more than to see people fail, it makes them look better. If you don't tell them where you're heading, they can't try to detour you or set up a roadblock.

Here is a catchphrase to be used as a reminder to show the world, before you tell it. "The steam that makes the whistle blow will never make the engine go."

Have you ever noticed a teapot heating on the stove just whistling and boiling away? Its power is going right out of the whistle spout. If you were to completely seal it up, one of two things would happen. One, it could use up all the water, and there would be no power at all. Or two, it would build up so much pressure, it would blow apart.

So what you must do is get some steam behind your purpose, your goals and plans, and abstain from throwing away your power by engaging in fruitless chitchat.

Again I emphasize, "Tell the world what you are going to do, but first show it." This alone will lessen the amount of negative talk you will have to ignore and overcome.

Victor Hugo (1802–1865) stated, "As a man or woman grows older and wiser, he or she talks less and says more." This is especially true as you hone your skills and start climbing the stairway to success. You will no longer feel the need to continually talk about what you plan to do, as you are now showing them.

All throughout this philosophy, I suggest and reiterate the following: "Thought, backed by strong desire, has a tendency to transmute itself into its physical equivalent." For our purpose of music and art, this means your thought, backed by your strong desire, will then transmute itself into its physical equivalent . . . which is your Plane of Success.

In your search for the secret of a method, do not look for a miracle, because you will not find it. You will find only the eternal laws of nature. These laws are available to you as long as you possess the *faith* and *courage* to use them. They may be used to bring freedom to an entire nation as well as deliver you to your Plane of Success.

Drumming Up 300,000,000 In Record Sales

Kenny Aronoff (World Class American drummer, sideman for numerous bands—live and in the studio, who has played on over 300 million records sold, and is probably best known for his work in The John Mellencamp band) has this advice. In his most influential book that chronicled his life for over a 35 year period, titled: *Sex, Drums, Rock 'n' Roll*, he stated, "I hope I can share with you the most important secret that I have learned: that there is no secret. It takes self-discipline, hard work, setting goals, communication skills, repetition, staying healthy, and staying relevant. It also helps to get lucky, but you can make a lot of luck by kicking rear-ends and not being a rear-end. I love playing the drums. I mean I really love it. And I get paid for it, which is simply bliss. Your business, whatever it is, might not last. But that doesn't mean your life is over, if you get anything out of my book, it's the fact that you have to keep trying and being the best you can be at whatever you do in life."

I would like to add to Kenny's plane of thought; "Where there is nothing to lose by trying and everything to gain if successful, by all means try." He also shares this example of "What it takes." This account of his dedication and commitment to be the best he could be is detailed here. He shares his method and process of learning, which might prove beneficial to you—my loyal *Think and Grow Through Art and Music* reader. He received a call from the Smashing Pumpkins band to fill in for their drummer. He said, "First I wrote out all of the drum parts, note for note. My approach is very methodical. I start memorizing five songs a day. The next day I review all of those songs and once I have them memorized, I start another five songs. On day three, I review all ten songs to make sure I have them memorized and then start learning five more. On day four, I review all fifteen songs and start learning five more. I do this until I have the entire set memorized. Repetition and persistence is the way I learn. There are no short cuts. I worked eight hours a day, taking only short breaks to eat and clear my mind. I felt like I was an actor learning a very heavy part in a movie and the movie was Smashing Pumpkins."

Eight hours per day until the job was complete is definitely the definition of Practice, Practice, Practice, as well as reinforcing two of my favorite necessities . . . *repetition* and *persistence*. Kenny has been and continues to be a true inspiration to thousands of upcoming drummers and musicians.

As Rob Swaynie of Indy Guitar professed: "There is a difference between a magician and a musician. There is no magic button to push. There is no fairy dust to spread about on your instrument that will guarantee success." Every artist I interviewed, including Rob Swaynie, agreed it is a definite necessity to **Practice, Practice, Practice**. These are three of the closest words to magic you will ever hear regarding reaching your Plane of Success. I could write an entire chapter on what I have been told regarding **Practice, Practice, Practice**.

The Sound of Music

Chet Atkins was very adamant that I share this essential trait of wisdom he had gained from his years of experience. He said, "Tell them to make sure they absolutely *'Love the sound of their instrument.'*" He emphasized the word *"love."* He said, "If they aren't *'in love'* with the sound it makes, get a different model or change instrument types all together. Maybe some *'love'* the sound of a keyboard or a horn, however are drawn to a guitar. I have seen some flourish after changing the instrument to meet their ear and heart." If you can hardly wait, and are overly anxious to get back to your chosen instrument to play it and hear the sound it generates, then you probably *"love it."* If not you might want to take a serious look and listen with your ear and heart to determine what is best for you. He spoke of the *"labor of love"* and the fact that if you are *"in love"* with the sound it makes, it's much easier and encouraging to practice for hours upon hours, day in and day out. The *"love"* of the sound and the *"labor of love"* are closely united.

The Sound of Romance

Here is a perfect example of the romantic nature of a man and his instrument stated rather poetically: Pepe Romero (Malaga, Spain— known for his technique and colorful musical interpretations of the classical and flamenco guitar) said this: "The guitar, by its very nature, the nature of its sound, by the soft nuance of its powerful and ancient voice, by the magic of the tone, goes directly to the part of oneself where *love* is felt. When I hear the sound of the guitar, it goes to some part inside of me that opens the door that holds feelings of love and everything beautiful that is inside of me. The love inside you manifests through sound, vibration and embraces everyone in the room." The love for your particular instrument and the love of the sound of your instrument is paramount.

Determination Determines Your Destination

The very first item of business regarding decision . . . you have to make a decision to Practice. Aristotle is quoted as saying, "We are what we repeatedly do. Excellence then is not an act, but a habit." In other words, given enough Practice, Practice, Practice . . . over time your act will no longer be seen as an act, however as a person of professional talent displaying excellence.

Just as I continually repeat myself throughout *Think and Grow Through Art and Music* for the purpose of learning, repetition is your key to becoming a master of your chosen instrument or art. In the genesis of your quest for excellence you will spend a great many more hours practicing than you will at performing. You must pay your dues. This is where you will need to organize your priorities. Does your burning desire have the upper hand on going to see one of your favorite movies just out at the theater? If you're a sports fan, does your burning desire override your sports desire to see your favorite team play? What if you were planning to practice for an audition of an event and suddenly your best friend says they have an all-expense-paid weekend to ski in Aspen? This is where your burning desire and self-determination should and will step-up and keep you focused on your path to success. Remind yourself that you are on a mission to do what needs to be done, and to do it within the time frame you've already established. There will be many times Practice, Practice, Practice will trump your recreational activities.

There is a story told regarding the famous jazz saxophonist, John Coltrane (1926–1967). It has been said he would sit for seven to eight hours straight, practicing just one scale. Then the very next day he would choose another scale and again sit and practice it seven to eight hours straight. Persistence? Yes!

Joe Pass (1929–1994) one of the greatest jazz guitarists of the twentieth century, had overwhelming practice discipline. Ironically Joe is who coined the phrase "Listen, Listen, Listen." He said at age ten he would practice seven to eight hours per day. He would practice two hours before school, two hours when he got home from school, then three to four hours each night. He not only Practiced, Practiced Practiced, he took it a step farther, he Listened, Listened, Listened. He remained vigilant at this ritual for nearly five years.

Do you have this kind of determination and are you willing to make this level of commitment to your instrument or art? Coltrane and Pass are an example, however it has somewhat been common practice for many professionals to take entire days perfecting their skills. Yo Yo Ma also made a very relevant point as well, when he said, "Practice everyday—Mastering music is more than learning technical skills. Practicing is about quality, not quantity. Some days I practice for hours; other days, just a few quality minutes on a very specific technique or exercise." In some cases quality out-ranks quantity.

Here is another example of determination. Gene Autry (1907–1998) The Singing Cowboy, Songwriter, Actor and Rodeo Performer—"I'm not a good actor, a good rider or a particularly good singer, however I am determined. I made a major decision at age twelve to buy a guitar. I saw one in the Sears & Roebuck catalog. I worked on my Uncle Calvin's farm, stacking and bailing hay. I finally saved the $8 I needed to buy that guitar. It was especially hard work for a wiry boy, but my ambition made me strong. It was my determination to get that guitar even though I was told I was too little to bale and stack hay, and man am I glad I stuck with it." Don't be ashamed of hard work or the type of job you need in order to earn the money required to buy your instrument or medium of art.

Definiteness of decision always requires courage and at times, very great courage. A person like you who reaches a definite decision to reach your Plane of Success, regardless of the cost, challenges, time, setbacks and efforts, not only stakes your reputation, you also stake your entire artistic life and freedom upon this decision.

By your desire to remain adamant, dutifully firm, and unwavering in your decisions, you have also adopted the principle of "Persistence" and "Never giving Up." Defeat may try to overtake you as it does many, but remember, defeat is never the same as failure until you accept it as such. You now understand that by looking at all defeat, as temporary defeat, you are able to make stepping stones out of what once appeared to be stumbling blocks.

There might come a time when you need to acquire a new found courage, a new vision and a new will to win. This takes Action. Action based on a Positive Mental Attitude. It was necessary for you to take Action to begin this journey, then Action to impel you along the way to keep going, and most importantly, Action to overcome temporary defeat by making a new or revised start if necessary.

If there comes a time when your results are not what you want them to be, examine your thoughts. What have you been thinking about on a daily basis? You will see that your results clearly match your thoughts. To change your results you must change your thoughts. Your outside world will eventually match your inner mental world perfectly.

Because you have *faith* and believe in yourself, you possess the power to turn every fear and worry, every feeling and every emotion into a positive driving ambition, to help you breeze into your Plane of Success.

There have been entire books written on the subject of "never giving up." In my opinion, there are none better than Sharon L. Lechter and Greg S. Reid's masterpiece *Three Feet from Gold*. This book is based on a Napoleon Hill story regarding a man who stopped three feet short of reaching a vein of gold, which would have yielded him a fortune. This book teaches many principles to overcome failure, including a Personal Success Equation. As I have been told, most musicians and artists eschew math, calculations and formulas, unless it relates to timing in a musical composition. However, please note, this formula introduced in *Three Feet from Gold*, could play a major role in your level of confidence and keep you on track to reach your Plane of Success.

$$[(P + T) \times A \times A] + F = \text{Your Personal Success}$$

Let me explain quite simply as they have instructed.

P is Passion. **T** is Talent. **A** is Associations. **A** is Action. **F** is Faith. When you combine your Passion and your Talent with right Associations and then take the right Action, you are well on your way to success. But to ensure you truly succeed and overcome any obstacles that may stand in your way, you need Faith. As they go on to further explain—Faith in yourself, your mission and your ability to succeed will help you persevere when times are difficult and propel you to even greater heights of success.

When you apply their formula to reaching your Plane of Success, you will find that giving up is not an option.

John Hiatt (American Singer-Songwriter), had this to say regarding passion; "They can't kill music. God knows they've tried, however music will always win as long as there's kids coming up that have a passion."

Here is Sir Ringo Starr's (English Singer-Songwriter, Actor and worldwide famous drummer for The Beatles) viewpoint: "My soul is that of a drummer . . . I didn't do it to become rich or famous. I did it out of passion for music and it was the love of my life."

I believe that since you have read this far into *Think and Grow Through Art and Music*, you not only have passion, you now possess a burning passion. So once again, integrate your passion and your talent with the most beneficial associations you can find then take Action to bring about that burning passion. Merely talking about it, will not bring about your passion, you must take Action!

THE PROFOUND PERCEPTION

Any dominating idea, plan or purpose held in the conscious mind through repetition of thought and emotionalized by a burning desire for its realization, is taken over by the subconscious and acted upon through whatever natural and logical means may be available.

Before closing this chapter on Decision, I would like to share one monumental reason why I think some are unable to, or don't want to make major decisions in their lives. It comes down to one word, "fear." In the majority of cases, if reaching a decision has been delayed, it's usually due to the fact that making this decision is going to bring you out of your comfort zone. You could possibly be suffering from the fear of change. In other words, you subconsciously understand that by making a certain decision, the consequences will affect changes in your daily life. As mentioned earlier, there are many who do not like change. Many like the comfort of just "playing it safe."

Let's say for example, you now realize and understand, that it is in fact "fear of change" that has you procrastinating in reaching a decision. Now that I have introduced the problem let's see if we can find a quick and easy solution.

First and foremost, make certain you have gathered and understand all of the facts surrounding this decision. You must have all the facts, both positive and negative to end up with the best decision. Realizing this is a major decision, and it most likely will alter your life and/or daily routine, you must look at the reality of how you will adapt to these changes. Making this decision will not only rid your mind of the fear, it will also prove to be most beneficial to your future.

In nearly every circumstance in my life, when I have made a life-changing decision, it has been for the good. This in turn brought a mammoth amount of freedom, to my psyche, like a five-hundred pound weight had been lifted from my shoulders.

Maybe this has happened to you at one time or another, if so remember when you made a major decision and how you immediately felt a calm and a level of confidence that you had done something good? Do you recall that feeling of success and saying, "Ah, yes, I finally . . .

When you're in doubt, remind yourself of that feeling, tell yourself by making this decision you will once again, feel that sense of accomplishment and success. Once you have made this decision and you know it's the correct decision, stand by it. Do Not Waver or Cave In.

The next chapter focuses on Persistence, which will help you understand why it's important to follow through with the decisions you make. The combination of making and standing by your decision, then being persistent in its pursuit, will further boost you to reaching your Plane of Success.

Chapter 7 QR Code Recap
Decision

Audio Only Duration 2:03 minutes

www.naphill.org/tgtam/chapter-7/

This QR Code excerpt was created by: Don M. Green, Executive Director and CEO of The Napoleon Hill Foundation Wise Virginia. A wealth of knowledge and a vast amount of material to help you reach your Plane of Success Available at: www.naphill.org

8
Persistence

*THE SUSTAINED EFFORT NECESSARY
TO INDUCE FAITH*

The Eighth Step Toward Reaching Your Plane of Success

Websters Dictionary defines persistence as: "The firm continuance in a course of action in spite of difficulty or opposition." Put another way: "Persistence is the ability to stick with something regardless of the boredom, challenges and negative influences." For example if you practice the violin for over a year to play "Twinkle, Twinkle, Little Star" perfectly, that is persistence.

Skill only comes from practice, patience and persistence. Calvin Coolidge (1872–1933) stated, "Nothing in the world can take the place of persistence. Talent will not; nothing is more common than unsuccessful men and women with talent. Genius will not; unrewarded genius is almost a proverb. Education will not; the world is full of educated derelicts. Persistence and determination alone are omnipotent." Said yet another way, persistence and determination combined have unlimited power. This combination is invincible and unconquerable.

Constant and determined effort will eventually break down any resistance and sweep away all obstacles.

Let's take two people for example. And let's say one has brilliance, but little patience. Let's say the other possesses little or average intelligence, but displays unwavering persistence. In nearly every case the latter is much more likely to reach their Plane of Success. "Sooner or later the man or woman who persists will win." If you have within your heart the ability to persist, then you already possess over fifty percent of what it takes to reach your Plane of Success. You are already half way there.

You will always be faced with life's challenges. Every person who has achieved greatness has had to overcome hurdles. For one who desires greatness, failure is unavoidable and part of the success formula. Think about the meaning of this famous quote: "Successful people often experience more failures, than failures do. However successful people manage to press on." Why is this? It's because failures give up.

I remind you now of a profound quote by Winston Churchill (1874–1965): "Never, never, never give up."

Jim Stovall (author of *The Ultimate Gift*, athlete, TV and movie producer, speaker, and recipient of The Humanitarian of The Year Award) states the following in his third volume of *Wisdom for Winners*.

"Research has shown that to become a world class master of any art or task, one must practice 10,000 hours. Most of these 10,000 hours of practice will involve immediate failure, identifying mistakes, recommitting our efforts and trying again. Don't try to avoid failure, use it to your advantage as an opportunity to do better. Don't stop and fail on your way to the top."

Harriet Beecher Stowe (1811–1896), American poet and author of *Uncle Tom's Cabin* put it this way: "When you get into a tight place and everything goes against you, until it seems as though you cannot hold on for another minute, don't give up there. This, is the place and time that the tide will turn." The tide will always turn in your favor if you are determined and don't give up.

Thomas Edison gave us this advice, "The most important factors of invention can be described in a few words. They consist first of explicit knowledge as to what one wishes to achieve. Next, you must fix your mind on that goal with persistence and begin searching for that which you seek, making use of all accumulated knowledge on the subject. You must keep on searching, no matter how many times you meet with disappointment. You must refuse to be influenced by the fact that someone else may have tried the same idea without success. You must keep yourself sold on the idea that the solution to your problem exists and you will find it."

The problem with most people is they quit before they start. In their thinking process as soon as one little roadblock or negative situation raises its head, they throw in the towel. Self-imposed limitations stop most people from ever beginning, because their thoughts turn negative. If they would only start, then keep going forward with a Positive Mental Attitude they would be surprised by their capabilities.

You either take possession of your mind and direct it toward the attainment of your goals, or your mind will take possession of you and give you whatever circumstance life happens to hand out. You will either become a "victim" or a "victor." You will either be more of a person or less of a person. The choice is yours to make. What do you prefer? How do you prefer to be known?

Just a reminder, Beethoven composed many of his masterpieces after the loss of his hearing. It would have made sense and been very easy for him to give up. Marian Anderson, born into poverty, had the loving support of her father who sold individual pieces of coal on the streets of Philadelphia to pay for her music lessons. She eventually went on to become one of America's most famous contraltos.

John Milton (1608–1674) had lost 100% of his eyesight by 1652. In 1667 he went on to write his most famous work, *Paradise Lost*, regarded as the greatest epic poem written in English.

Abraham Lincoln (1809–1865) had persisted and put forth undying effort to gain the presidency of the United States, however had to borrow money for transportation to his own inauguration.

When Henry Ford was following his Definite Major Purpose, which was to build a horseless carriage, he was faced with many challenges. Not only did he experience every form of discouragement, humility and public criticism, he also had to overcome legal hurdles. A police ordinance was passed making it illegal to operate his self-propelled vehicle on many streets, because it spooked the horses. Now I ask you, do you think he let this stop him?

Willpower and desire, when properly combined, make an irresistible pair. In so many instances the majority of people will give up, take on new direction or just quit all together when the wind of challenge blows against them. For some it only takes a breeze. At the first sign of opposition and having to prevail, they throw in the towel.

However, those who become successful, like you, will carry on despite any and all opposition until reaching your Plane of Success. Remaining vigilant, without retreat, allows you to overcome fear, doubt and negativity.

One of my favorite all time quotes is from the late Reverend Robert H. Schuller, who hosted the *Hour of Power* television program for forty years. "Tough times never last, tough people do." To my knowledge there has never been an accomplished or creatively gifted person who hasn't known some level of despair, frustration, tough times or failure. We already know tough times never last, neither does despair, frustration nor failure. There will be periods when fresh ideas, inspiration and the creative juices don't seem to flow. There might be times, like with Abraham Lincoln, when money seemed non-existent.

The secret here is to first go back, read your mission statement aloud. See and feel yourself already arriving at your Plane of Success. Empathize when you come to the part of your mission statement, "*I will let nothing stop me.*" In some circumstances this is all that is required to get you back on track.

Your first test as to your persistence will come when you begin to follow the six steps outlined in Chapter Two, Faith. Not only is lack of persistence one of the most common causes of failure; it is also one of the most common weaknesses in men and women. It is a weakness that can be overcome by effort. The intensity of your burning desire will dictate how easily lack of persistence can and will be conquered. As you recall, desire is the starting point of all achievement.

Dr. Hill uses this analogy: "Weak desires bring weak results, just as a small amount of fire makes a small amount of heat." If you find yourself lacking in persistence, this weakness may be overcome by building a stronger and bigger fire under your desires. You need to make sure you are not only passionate about your desire, you also need to be "excited" with the realization that you will, one day, reach your Plane of Success. Your enthusiasm is what kindles your fire. Flaming enthusiasm, backed up by horse sense and unwavering persistence, is the quality that makes for success.

If and when you find yourself beginning to drift, or fearful, or filled with doubt, is when you will need countermeasures. This first countermeasure is to re-visit Autosuggestion. Again, re-affirm your desire by repeating your mission statement. This paragraph has the ability to influence your subconscious mind by bringing you a clearer image of your Plane of Success. Your subconscious mind works continuously, while you are awake, and especially while sleeping. At this point it is also necessary to surround yourself with your Master Mind alliance. There is an entire chapter dedicated to this most beneficial and indispensable part of the success philosophy. It will be explained in detail in an upcoming chapter. The simple definition of the Master Mind alliance is; "The coordination of knowledge and effort in a spirit of harmony, between two or more people, for the attainment of a definite purpose." By using the cooperative efforts of the members of your Master Mind alliance you will be able to develop and maintain persistence.

Maintaining Your Momentum

When "mother doubt" raises her fearful head and you begin to question your own abilities, you will need to reboot your level of confidence. It might be necessary to start slow at first, and then increase your speed until you finally gain complete and total control over your will. Starting to rebuild your confidence slowly should not be seen as a handicap or weakness, however a sign of strength with the understanding that persistence, regardless of its speed, will bring you to your Plane of Success. This means starting exactly where you are today, at this moment, and not waiting for life to create the circumstances you think you need to succeed. It means taking the first step now, which could be reading your mission statement again. Then taking another step, which could be consulting your Master Mind alliance. This will lead to another step until you find yourself at a speedy pace. There is no set speed for persistence, it is consistent and when you realize the power it yields by remaining in perpetual motion at all times, you will be that much closer to reaching your Plane of Success. As Dr. Martin Luther King Jr. (1929–1968) stated, "If you can't fly, run, if you can't run, then walk, and if you can't walk, crawl, but what ever you do, you must keep moving forward always."

I asked Keiko Matsui (Japanese Jazz-Jazz fusion Keyboardist and Composer), if there was a time that she felt like giving up and if so, what kept her going? She replied, "Yes, when I took time off to have a baby, I lost confidence and my focus had shifted from music to family. It was my fans who helped me regain confidence in myself by telling me I had a great talent and asked me to please come back." Here is a person with a tremendous amount of talent being sidelined by her own thoughts. It was the encouragement and inspiration of others who steered her back to being her persistent self, allowing her to continue to follow her dreams.

If and when you become complacent or unfocused, try to recall what someone has said to you that buoyed your level of confidence. Repeat those inspiring words over and over. Write them down so your brain can see them. By reiterating just these few words, it can have the same effect as the one sentence that brought Keiko Matsui back into the limelight she enjoys today. Be Persistent. No matter how slowly you start at first, always remember: "With Persistence Will Come Success."

A motivated person such as yourself understands there will always be difficulties to overcome. You understand you must face these challenges head on. You must remain steadfast, resourceful and resilient enough to counteract and overcome these challenges. This is accomplished by persistence and persistence alone. When you remain persistent you never even consider the costs. Your major purpose is liable to lead you right through the lions den or Death Valley in July. By remaining persistent, all other considerations remain secondary to your major purpose and reaching your Plane of Success.

As I've mentioned there is no such thing as something for nothing. No sailing right to the top without hard work and persistence. There will be times when you are met with "Mr. Misfortune" over and over again. He is merely a test. A test of your tenacity. A test to see if you really have what it takes to reach your Plane of Success. A test to see if you can continue to overcome the misfortunes and challenges laid before you. In the majority of cases there is no hope of reaching your greatness without being met face on by Mr. Misfortune. Your challenge lies in your ability to forge right ahead, knowing by remaining vigilant you are on the way, and you will reach your desired Plane of Success. It is important to understand how this quote "Every adversity carries with it the seed of an equivalent benefit or greater," plays a role in conquering failure due to a lack of persistence. By reaching your Plane of Success through persistence, and overcoming all adversities, you will come to know, understand, and embrace the above thirteen words of hope and confidence.

The Seed of Adversity Test

The thirteen words mentioned above, are one of those truths I spoke of earlier, that never need variation. I would like to concrete these thirteen words by an example. Many learn from example, so try this:

Take a moment to look back in your past and analyze the times you have faced defeat. Bring that adverse or unpleasant situation into focus. Chances are if it were far enough back in your past, then the wound has had time to heal and you can find the good that came from it. Now think carefully, can you see a positive result that came from this misfortune? Sometimes you have to look hard and in depth. The seed of an equivalent benefit or greater does not always appear immediately. Sometimes it takes weeks, months and possibly years. Sometimes the benefit can simply be, learning one of life's essential lessons. If you look hard enough with your, newly formed Positive Mental Attitude, in ninety-five percent of all cases, it will appear. Can you see it? Now you ask, what good does this do me now? It's the confidence booster. It's a concrete fact you can rely on the very next time you face adversity. Knowing that some good will come from misfortune and this knowledge will help you bolster your life in any arena.

Training Yourself To Be Persistent

Napoleon Hill makes it perfectly clear that persistence is a state of mind and can be developed by anyone. He gives us a list of eight fundamental ingredients required in training your mind to remain persistent.

1. **Definiteness of purpose.** Knowing what you want is the first and, perhaps, the most important step toward the development of persistence. A strong motive will force you to surmount many difficulties.

2. **Desire.** It is comparatively easy to acquire and to maintain persistence in pursuing the object of your intense desire.

3. **Self-reliance.** Belief in your ability to carry out a plan will encourage you to follow the plan through with persistence. (Self-reliance can be developed through the principle described in the chapter on Auto-suggestion).

4. **Definiteness of plans.** Organized plans, even though they may be weak and entirely impractical in the beginning, encourage persistence.

5. **Accurate knowledge.** Knowing that your plans are sound, based upon experience or observation, encourages persistence; "guessing" instead of "knowing" destroys persistence.

6. **Cooperation.** Sympathy, understanding, and harmonious cooperation with others tend to develop persistence.

7. **Will-power.** The habit of concentrating your thoughts upon the building of plans for the attainment of a definite purpose leads to persistence.

8. **Habit.** Persistence is the direct result of habit. Your mind absorbs and becomes a part of the daily experiences upon which it feeds. Fear, the worst of all enemies, can be effectively cured by *forced repetition of acts of courage.*

Here it is important to take an inventory of which, if any, of these eight fundamental ingredients you are lacking. Be brave and dauntless in your personal assessment. Understand every word and every definition. This is extremely important, as this report card will reveal to you certain areas, which require immediate attention. Persistence is based upon definite causes. We need to make sure you have a grip on these causes before we move on. Take an honest inventory now. Can you identify with any areas in which you lack?

Once again it is just as important to know the causes of "lack of persistence" as it is to know and understand what it takes to develop "persistence." Dr. Hill has given us sixteen real enemies, which stand between you and noteworthy achievement. He not only gives us the "symptoms" indicating weakness of persistence, he also explains the deeply seated subconscious causes of this weakness.

If you really wish to know who you are and what you truly are capable of, take inventory of yourself.

These are the weaknesses and true enemies you must conquer to reach your Plane of Success.

1. Failure to recognize and to define clearly exactly what you want.
2. Procrastination, with or without cause. (Usually backed up with a formidable array of alibis and excuses.)
3. Lack of interest in acquiring specialized knowledge.
4. Indecision; the habit of "passing the buck" on all occasions, instead of facing issues squarely. (Also backed by alibis.)
5. The habit of relying upon alibis instead of creating definite plans for the solution of problems.
6. Self-satisfaction; There is but little remedy for this affliction, and no hope for those who suffer from it.
7. Indifference; usually reflected in your readiness to compromise on all occasions, rather than meet opposition and fight it.
8. The habit of blaming others for your mistakes, and accepting unfavorable circumstances as being unavoidable.

9. Weakness of desire, due to neglect in the choice of motives that impel action.

10. Willingness, even eagerness, to quit at the first sign of defeat. (Based upon one or more of the six basic fears.)

11. Lack of organized plans, placed in writing where they may be analyzed.

12. The habit of neglecting to move on ideas, or to grasp opportunity when it presents itself.

13. Wishing instead of willing.

14. The habit of compromising with failure instead of aiming at your Plane of Success. General absence of ambition to *be*, to *do*, to *own*.

15. Searching for all the short-cuts to success, trying to get, without giving a fair equivalent.

16. Fear of criticism; failure to create plans and to put them into action, because of what other people will think, do, or say. This enemy belongs at the head of the list, because it generally exists in one's subconscious mind, where its presence is not recognized. (See the Six Basic Fears in a later chapter.)

They Say! Who Are They?

Let's examine number sixteen in detail. To a large part, the majority of people have a strong tendency to allow the thoughts and beliefs of others to influence their capacity for success. It's usually those closest to us, or those we look up to who can do the most damage. Our friends, relatives and business associates, have so much influence over our lives. At times we cannot think, live, strive and go forth in a spirit of confidence due to the fear of their criticism. When constantly worrying about what "they say," it sometimes holds us back from stepping out into risky areas. This fear of criticism creates one of the major failures of success. This is one of the biggest reasons why some people *never even begin to try*. This is why when some are met with temporary failure, they have the habit of giving up. They don't want someone to say something like; "Look at that fool, they keep trying the impossible." It's that fear of criticism, which keeps many from even starting. It's that fear of a person, uneducated in the philosophy of success, who might say something to hurt our feelings, or tell us we are not capable of achieving our desire, that can be the most detrimental. These fears have stopped many dead in their tracks. Don't listen to what "they say."

Conquering What "They Say"

Here is a perfect example of how the fear of criticism stopped many athletes. In 1945, medical authorities reported that it was impossible to run a mile in less than four minutes, because the human heart was not capable. Therefore a man or woman would be a fool to attempt such a feat that could possibly bring death. Roger Bannister (1929–2018) was different. He did not believe what "they said." You might have heard his story. As part of his training, he relentlessly visualized running a mile in less than four minutes. He said he visualized the achievement in order to create a sense of certainty in his mind and body. In 1954, he was the first person to break the four-minute mile barrier. Can you guess? Shortly thereafter there were suddenly more runners who no longer listened to what "they said." They too broke the barrier. In a period of a little more than four years after he first broke the four-minute mile, the feat was accomplished 46 more times by Roger and other runners. In one race in 1958, in Dublin, Ireland, five runners finished in just under four minutes. What had changed? Their mental perception had changed, and the fact that they would no longer be looked upon as a fool for trying. There were no scientific or running technique breakthroughs, only the mental breakthrough of what people now believed was possible.

Are you listening to what "they say?" Are the voices playing in your head "theirs," or are they your own positive . . . "I know I can do this and I will let nothing stop me" . . . voice?

To overcome what "they say," one beneficial technique is just to look at what others have accomplished. Were they also told they couldn't achieve their desires and goals? Were they told they would never make it or they weren't good enough or didn't come from the right background, etc.?

They might have been showered with negativity, however, they had an unnerving belief in themselves and therefore were able to overcome what "they said." They were unaffected by the criticism because they had a definite purpose in life and their definite purpose continued to drive them forward and that drive remained a matter of the utmost importance to them.

The next time you experience doubt or fear and say things to yourself like, "I don't think I can do this," stop for a minute and ask yourself why? Ask yourself if this negative belief or thought came from something someone said to you, something you heard on the radio, something you read in the paper or something a friend or relative said. Once you pinpoint the origin of this thought or belief, you will then understand and see once again, it is what "they said." It's not your thought, so do not let it occupy your mind. Repeat your mission statement immediately and just see what happens. You will quickly see your mind is stronger than theirs and your thoughts will prevail. Also stop again and think about those who have already accomplished and reached their Plane of Success. If they can do it, you can do it.

How To Develop Persistence

Dr. Hill gives us four simple steps, which lead to the habit and development of persistence. They call for no great amount of intelligence, no particular amount of education, and but little time or effort. The necessary steps are:

1. A definite purpose backed by burning desire for its fulfillment.
2. A definite plan, expressed in continuous action.
3. A mind closed tightly against all negative and discouraging influences, including negative suggestions of relatives, friends and acquaintances.
4. A friendly alliance with one or more persons who will encourage you to follow through with both your plan and purpose.

These four steps are essential for success in all walks of life. As a matter of fact, the entire purpose of the 13 principles toward reaching your Plane of Success is to enable you to take these four steps as a matter of habit.

John D. Rockefeller (1839–1937) said, "I do not think there is any other quality so essential to success other than persistence. It overcomes almost everything, even nature."

THE PROFOUND PERCEPTION

Any dominating idea, plan or purpose held in the conscious mind through repetition of thought and emotionalized by a burning desire for its realization, is taken over by the subconscious and acted upon through whatever natural and logical means may be available.

Understanding the Six Letter "F" Word

I cannot leave this essential chapter on persistence without going into greater detail on the word "Failure." To the uneducated, the word failure, means nothing other than negativity. As soon as the uneducated person hears or sees the word failure, he or she will automatically say or think, "It's over and finished." For those of us who stand by W. Clement Stone's acronym **PMA, "Positive Mental Attitude,"** it means just the opposite. Failure is success. Yes, by failing we have successfully found out what did not work. It's just the same as when an assistant to Thomas Edison proclaimed; "We're wasting time, we've tried over ten thousand times and still haven't found the right material to create the incandescent light." However, Edison with his **PMA** attitude said, "Aha, but now we know over ten thousand things which will not work, which means we're getting closer." Success is not accomplished by not failing; it is accomplished by not giving up.

Eminem (American Rapper, Record Producer, and Actor), spoke of adversity by saying; "If people take anything from my music, it should be motivation to know that anything is possible as long as you keep working hard and don't back down."

In the field of art and music there are always references made to the words genius, talent, prodigy and luck in playing a role in one's artistic ability and success. You must realize that one who is in possession of any of these characteristics, without some level of persistence, which is driven by a definite aim or purpose . . . will in no way assure he or she will ever reach their Plane of Success.

Most real failures and shortcomings come about, due to the limitation you set up in your own mind. It is noteworthy to write the following words down, where you can see them often. "The only limitations I have, are the one's I set up in my own mind." When you conquer your own mind you can achieve anything. It is similar to putting the proper fuel into a vehicle; you need to fuel your brain with the proper thoughts.

As in *Three Feet from Gold*, if a person had *courage* to go a few steps further, they might discover the key that opens the door leading to their Plane of Success.

Riding With The King

I feel compelled to share another common cause of failure in today's world. In some genres of music you have probably heard the famous adage "Sex, Drugs and Rock 'n' Roll." Mississippi born, B.B. King (1925–2015), the famous blues guitarist, was asked the following question: What piece of advice would you give to a younger person who aspires to become a professional musician? Without giving much thought, he said, "For Gods sake, tell them to stay away from those damned drugs. I have seen more talent wasted and thrown out the window from drugs. First they experiment and then they are hooked. They either end up with an overdose or their fellow players get so tired of dealing with them, that they quit." He said, "sooner or later, they end up going up Broadway the wrong direction." He also shares a story of playing in a Florida prison where one of his daughters was held there on a drug conviction.

I have interviewed others who mention the abuse of alcohol as a contributing factor in ruining a person's career and life.

Help

If you see yourself slipping away or getting caught up, then for your sake, your family's sake, and the sake of your fellow associates . . . seek **HELP**. The entire planet is dotted with care facilities and recovery centers. One boasting a successful rate of rehabilitation is Eric Clapton's Crossroads. Located away from the confusion of life in addiction, Crossroads is on the island of Antigua.

If drugs and/or alcohol are controlling or starting to control your life, do not be embarrassed, reach out and seek help now.

Friending Failure

In her excellent book on winning, *Go For It,* Dr. Irene C. Kassorla, shrink to the Hollywood stars, states: "Winners make friends with failure and acknowledge the valuable lessons that it teaches. Failures offer valuable information and are helpful guides, not signals to give up. Failure is a part of the success pattern and no one achieves their goals in one straight climb. It's more like a jagged, uneven ascent with curves and plateaus." Please note her words: "Not signals to give up." Sooner or later we all meet head on with failure. Your greatest, strongest and most powerful tool, known to mankind, is the power of your own mind. The good news is that you are the one in complete and total control of this most powerful tool. It lies at your beck and call. You guide its thoughts, thereby creating its outcome.

Confucius (551–479 B.C.) said, "A man or woman is great not because he or she hasn't failed: they are great because failure hasn't stopped them." The old Japanese proverb simply says, "Fall seven times, stand up eight."

Madonna went to NYC with thirty-five dollars in her pocket. She worked at Dunkin Donuts. After being turned down dramatically by Millennium Records, she said something inside of her told her to not give up. This rejection motivated her to continue working even harder. Finally she got a record deal with Seymour Stein of Sire Records. Stein recalled meeting Madonna and saying, "I believed in her, because not only did she have talent, she had a *burning desire,* drive, ambition, and a work ethic that was incredible." Note his use of the words, *Burning Desire.*

Can you recall an example of a time when you were faced with failure, however you remained persistent and displayed that . . . "I'm not giving up attitude," until you succeeded? Do you remember how it felt? Did you puff your chest out and say, "Yes, I knew I could do it." Do you remember the joy? This is the exact feeling you will have when reaching your Plane of Success by remaining persistent and ignoring failure . . . except tenfold.

From this day forward, look at all failure as an inspiration and a challenge to overcome. When you look at failure with conviction and renewed *faith* this will buoy you and strengthen your level of confidence, which will deliver you to your Plane of Success.

Chapter 8 QR Code Recap

Persistence   Audio Only Duration 9:36 minutes

This QR Code excerpt was created by: Don M. Green, Executive Director and CEO of The Napoleon Hill Foundation Wise Virginia. A wealth of knowledge

www.naphill.org/tgtam/chapter-8/   and a vast amount of material to help

you reach your Plane of Success

Available at: www.naphill.org

9
The Power of
the Master Mind

THE DRIVING FORCE

The Ninth Step Toward Reaching
Your Plane of Success

A Master Mind alliance is built of two or more minds working actively together in perfect harmony toward a common definite object. No one mind has ever attained outstanding success in any field without applying the principle of the Master Mind.

They might not have referred to it as the Master Mind, but the fact that they conspired with one or more to attain their success is the same principle. No one mind is totally complete by itself. All truly great minds have been reinforced through contact with others thereby pooling their resources and allowing them to grow, merge and expand.

Although this Master Mind principle has found its success in every aspect within the world of business and finance, I will explain how it will also be of great benefit to you, as you *Think and Grow Through Art and Music.*

Today you might liken your Master Mind alliance to members of your symphony, members of your band, fellow associates at your recording studio, or others working in the field of art. In other words you and your fellow members are striving and aspiring to attain a spirit of harmony within the confines of your given genre. You are all striving for a common goal.

To explain this in further detail: The Master Mind principle is the principle in which you may borrow and use the education, influence, wisdom and experience of other people which in turn will aid you in reaching your Plane of Success. It is a principle that you can use to accomplish more in one year than you could in an entire lifetime, if you were to rely on your efforts alone. Isn't it a wonderful concept to realize you can enjoy and use other's education, know-how and skills, when you form a Master Mind alliance with them? Please note; there must be an equal benefit for them as well, making it possible for them to also attain that which they desire.

Woodrow Wilson (1856–1924), once said, "I not only use all the brains I have, but all that I can borrow."

Here are 3 steps to aid in setting up your Master Mind alliance:

One. Decide and write down exactly where you see yourself during the next three years.

Two. Decide exactly what you plan to give in return for reaching this three-year goal. How will you guide your efforts?

Three. Form a Master Mind alliance with a family member or one other person, who will work with you in a spirit of harmony and who will also benefit by reaching your goal.

An active alliance of two or more minds in a spirit of perfect harmony for the attainment of a common objective stimulates each mind to a higher degree of courage than is ordinary and paves the way for that state of mind known as *faith*.

When two or more people have a common purpose, and act in a spirit of harmony in attaining their common purpose, they will develop the necessary courage and *faith to achieve their goal*.

Your Greatest Source of Power Scientifically Explained

I suggest reading this slowly and with much consideration. Explained here is a major key that will aid you in understanding how to make this philosophy work. Without getting too technical and scientific, we must take a look at Physics. First, research has proven that matter and energy are interchangeable. Invented between 1929 and 1934, the cyclotron is a particle accelerator. It accelerates charged sub-atomic particles to high speeds using a powerful magnetic field. When this is broken down, what we once thought was solid matter, actually releases energy. Energy is nature's universal set of building blocks. Everything in our entire universe is made of this energy. Through a process we may one day completely understand, nature changes energy into matter and reverses the process.

When two or more minds blend their thinking in a spirit of harmony and work toward the same end goal, they place themselves in a position, through this blending, to absorb power directly from the great universal storehouse of *Infinite Intelligence*. This is the greatest of all sources of power. Thought is a form of energy. This energy far exceeds the energy derived from the atom, because our energy is within our control and we are capable of directing it. This is the highest form of creative effort known to man and its potential can be mind-boggling.

How does all this apply to us? The set of nature's building blocks, I referred to are available in the form of thought energy!

We do know the human brain is both a receiver and a broadcasting station for the vibrations of thought. It's very similar to a radio broadcasting & receiving set. We know that when two or more minds have been aroused and warmed in a spirit of harmony and enthusiasm, there is a meeting of the minds, and this meeting steps up the vibrations of each mind. This means each person in the group will tune in and have the benefit of this higher vibration.

Here is a very important fact to grasp. The spiritual benefit of this group effort equals to a naked truth: no two minds ever come together without, thereby, creating a third, invisible and intangible force which may be likened to a third and completely separate mind. This spirit of harmony creates increased energy that becomes available to every member of the group. Napoleon described it as the "psychic" phase of the Master Mind alliance.

Another example can be stated this way, "If I give you one of my dollars for one of yours, each of us will have not profited, but, if I give you one of my thoughts in return for one of your thoughts, each of us has gained one hundred percent dividend on our investment." You most likely have heard the expressions—"Two heads are better than one," or "The whole is greater than the sum of its individual parts."

Since Andrew Carnegie first called attention to the power of a Master Mind, intense research into the cause of this power has been carried out. The minds of thousands have been systematically explored and their reactions to thought stimuli have been examined. The results are monumental in proving the existence of this Master Mind principle.

A scientific explanation would be H_2O. As we all know H_2O equals water. Both hydrogen and oxygen are gases in their natural state, however, their combination is not a gas but a liquid. We have two parts hydrogen and one part oxygen. The two parts hydrogen by themselves are just that . . . two parts hydrogen. The one part oxygen by itself, is just that . . . one part oxygen. However, when blended together, like our human minds, they create a third component, something completely different . . . water.

Everyday table salt is another good example. Salt, used sparingly, is basically harmless, even necessary for our bodies. However, by separating its components from their original state, we get the volatile elements of sodium and chloride.

Another example, would be comparing our human brains to a set of electric batteries. We understand as fact that a group of batteries will provide more energy than a single battery. We also understand as fact that an individual battery will provide energy in the direct proportion to the number and capacity of the cells it contains. Our brains function in much the same way. This is why some brains are more efficient than others. This brings us to the profound understanding—a group of brains coordinated (or connected) in a spirit of harmony will provide more thought-energy than a single brain, just as the group of batteries provide more energy than a single battery.

Therefore, the Master Mind alliance, in a spirit of harmony for the attainment of a purpose, provides energy that is the equivalent of all the individual batteries connected, so that their combined power is available through one source.

What does all this prove? Very simply put:

1. The nature of matter can be changed by changing the relationships of its components and elements; and
2. The nature of thought can be modified and changed by the alliance of two or more minds.

Understanding this principle explains why some with little or no formal schooling can rise to the top of their field, or play in a very successful ensemble. This provides explanations for many of the unknown or unexplainable prosperity surrounding the fields of art and music.

I keep mentioning this "Spirit of Harmony" due to its most relevant nature. There must be harmony within the relationships in the minds of your Master Mind alliance. It is very similar to the harmony in music, which are simultaneously reoccurring frequencies of tones and chords. Without the factor of harmony, the alliance will be nothing more than ordinary cooperation or just a friendly coordination of effort.

Ralph Waldo Emerson (1803–1882) said, "Every institution is a lengthened shadow of one man." What is he saying here? He is alluding to the fact that success cannot be attained alone. (It takes more than one to boogie.) You cannot experience and/or use this increased energy without a complete and free "Spirit of Harmony."

Likewise, if your group for some reason has conflict where there is a spirit of *Disharmony*, then the increased energy can bring about major frustration. This in turn will negate your goal as a group and make it much slower and difficult to accomplish, if at all. It's true there needs to be a leader, or coordinator in the group, however, this does not mean the leader's thoughts would dominate and/or subdue the thoughts of another group member. When one person tries to dominate the group, it sets the stage for rebellion and resistance. It might not be open rebellion, however, it is rebellion in the mind, which can and usually will cause discord within your alliance.

Andrew Carnegie's Master Mind Strategy

You recall that Mr. Carnegie is the visionary who realized a philosophy needed to be developed, such as, the one you are now studying. I give you an example of how discord within your alliance, can be resolved by sharing this Andrew Carnegie Master Mind scenario.

He knew very little regarding the details of making, selling and distributing steel. He did not pretend to know. However, he did have a cast of men working for him who understood every aspect surrounding the steel business. When he first entered the business, steel was selling for $140 per ton. This was a substantial amount of money in the early 1900s. He knew if he could lower the price he could create an empire. He assembled his Master Mind alliance and together they were able to reduce the price to $20 per ton. This made steel an every day commodity and paved the way to change the infrastructure and appearance of every city in the United States as well as the entire landscape of the country. He was truly the father of the steel age.

Now that I've set the groundwork, here is how he dealt with an example of discord discovered in his Master Mind alliance. He wanted to locate the very best trained person in the world to be his head chemist, so he sent out a "headhunter" to find such a person. This leading chemist was found in Germany. Mr. Carnegie drew up a contract on a five-year basis, however, by the end of the first year, they discovered that he could not work in harmony with the other members of Mr. Carnegie's Master Mind alliance. Due to his temperament, this celebrated chemist was discharged at the end of the first year. Mr. Carnegie paid him and sent him on his way.

Mr. Carnegie made this profound statement in saying that one single person with a negative mental attitude, allowed to intermix in a factory of a thousand people, could discolor their minds without saying a word. This is a bold statement, however a statement coming from such an ingenious judge of character as Andrew Carnegie, is most deserving of our attention.

It's important to understand why he said one person with a negative attitude can influence a thousand others without saying a word. It is a well-known fact that people with a disagreeable mental attitude will disturb every person with whom they associate. They will do this by their state of mind alone, without speaking a word or making even so much as a disagreeable gesture of any nature. This person, with this type of mental attitude, can merely enter the room and a large portion of those in attendance will become uncomfortable. This powerful influence can work the other way as well. When a person enters the room with a pleasing, positive, enthusiastic and harmonious mental attitude, they create a pleasant atmosphere, which ushers in comfort, calmness and vibrations of confidence. The scientific term of this awareness is called *Telepathy.* Webster defines telepathy as: Communication from one mind to another by extrasensory means.

It is through telepathy that one mind can reach out to thousands. (I will have more input on this later.) Your mind is constantly in tune with every mind around you within its range. Some minds have a longer range than others. This is why you cannot afford to remain in a negative atmosphere. I will give you techniques in a subsequent chapter to protect you from this.

The Most Powerful Master Mind Alliance On This Planet

One of the best examples, as well as the most powerful Master Mind alliance to date, is the embodiment of The United States of America. It is through this highly regarded alliance that the freedom enjoyed within the United States remains intact today, just as it did when those fifty-six men gave the nation its birthright of liberty and freedom by signing their names to the Declaration of Independence. The strength of this alliance has its seat in the fact that it is voluntary and is supported by the people in a spirit of harmony.

There is no single person or single mind, no matter how powerful, that could have given the United States the vision, and the self-reliance, by which its leaders in all walks of life have been inspired.

To take this one step further, let's look at the Presidency of the United States. What might seem like disharmony at times, is actually harmony in the respect that the President works in conjunction with the members of the cabinet, as well as a great number of other advisors. Without the aid of this alliance, there would be extreme difficulty in leading the United States.

A Master Mind Orchestra

Daniel Barenboim (Grammy Winner; Gramophone Hall of Fame Pianist and Conductor; Past Music Conductor of The Chicago Symphony Orchestra, The Orchestre de Paris and La Scala in Milan; a citizen of Argentina, Israel, Palestine and Spain), said "I am the conductor for life of the Staats Kapelle in Berlin, which fills me with tremendous joy because I feel absolutely at one with them. When we play, I have a feeling that together we manage to create one collective lung for the whole orchestra so that everybody on the stage 'breathes' the music in and out the same way."

Don't you find Mr. Barenboim's words quite poetic, as he ushers in the exact nucleus of a true Master Mind alliance by all breathing in sync as one?

Master Mind Duos

"If it is true that a woman may 'make' or 'break' a man, it is true because of woman's mystic power in the spirit of romance with which she may lift a man high, or drive him down to the depths of despair."

—ROSA LEE BEELAND HILL

As previously mentioned, perhaps the number one, most logical and most powerful Master Mind alliance, is that of a husband and a wife. Both Henry Ford and Thomas Edison credit their wives to being the driving forces in their Master Mind alliances.

Edgar Winter (American multi-instrumentalist, singer-songwriter) said this regarding his alliance: "The most profound tangible influence in my life has been my wife, Monique. I don't know that I would even be alive were it not for her, and I certainly would not be the person I am today."

Another prime example are these song-writing teams which have also created two-person Master Mind alliances. Each pair worked together as partners for a common cause; Lennon/McCartney, Rogers/Hammerstein, Elton John/Bernie Taupin, Carole King/Gerry Goffin, Jagger/Richards, George/Ira Gershwin, Felice and Boudleaux Bryant, Jerry Leiber/Mike Stoller, and Burt Bacharach/Hal David. These are just a few of the many song-writing duos that have collaborated in a spirit of harmony.

Specific Mini-Master Mind Alliances
THE IMPORTANCE OF SEEKING CONSTRUCTIVE CRITICISM

In his highly acclaimed and landmark work *The Big Gig* (A one hundred percent must read) Zoro ("The Minister of Groove" and one of the world's most respected drummers), shares this story regarding criticism. He said, in most cases it's fear and pride that causes reluctance in musicians seeking constructive criticism. He says this is a huge mistake. He suggests asking the musicians you are playing with if they can suggest or see any areas in your playing that needs improvement. By getting their honest opinions it gives you a blueprint of what you need to work on the most. You must humble yourself to receive the feedback you need. Zoro claims that this approach helped him improve more than any other previous tactic. He states, "No matter where you are in your career, if you truly want to continue to grow and develop as an artist and musician, you must welcome critique from your peers and experts." Stephen Covey said, "It takes humility to ask for feedback. It takes wisdom to understand it, analyze it, and appropriately act on it."

In order to continually improve, you must level with the other players and tell them why you desire their feedback. It's essential to tell them you are looking for ways to improve any and all aspects of your playing as well as your participation within the group. This way it will make it easier for them to give you an honest report rather than one they might think you want to hear.

I share the following with you, especially if you are a drummer, so that you can understand and embrace the power of asking for advice. Zoro stated that he asked this question to one of the professional musicians in a band he was drumming with; "What can I do to increase my chances of becoming a successful musician?" He was told that the most important thing you can learn as a drummer, is to play in the groove, any groove, no matter how simple it is, and make it feel great. He was urged to play regularly with a metronome. He was told not to change the groove—don't alter it, don't do one fill, don't change anything—just play the same groove with the metronome for ten minutes straight and to sit on that groove until it was smooth as silk, until it's flawless. Zoro said this was the turning point for him as a drummer as it caused a paradigm shift in his thinking. Asking for advice pays off. When the time is right, humble yourself and ask for help.

Creating A Master Mind Alliance

First you must determine the exact purpose in creating this particular Master Mind alliance. Are you forming this alliance to complete a specific goal or are you forming this alliance to work toward your Definite Major Purpose in life?

If you are creating this alliance to accomplish a specific goal, then you can be much more specific in the particular characteristics of the members you choose. If you are forming this alliance to work toward your Definite Major Purpose in life, then you will have a broader scope of individuals to choose from, as you look farther into the distance.

Next you should have a basic idea of exactly what you hope to accomplish with the members you choose for your alliance. I also suggest that you always keep an open mind, because your direction and your end goal can sometimes shift.

Choose members whose training, experience, and skill set make them the most beneficial in achieving the goals of your alliance. You don't have to accept the first person who meets your requirements, it's best to interview several before making your final decision. In a way, you can liken this process as if you were judging auditions. How well do they fit? They need ability, personality and willingness to cooperate with your group.

It is paramount to establish exactly what benefit each member may receive in return for their congenial cooperation. It is important to be fair and generous. The more generous you are, the more pleasing cooperation you will receive from them.

Next you will all need to agree on a place and a time to meet. You must keep in constant contact with your alliance. There should be no secrets between you.

When you have established perfect harmony between your mind and the minds of the others in your Master Mind alliance, you will discover that ideas will flash in your mind and the minds of the others. These ideas would normally not come to one mind or your mind alone. You must be able to see clearly that you can work in a spirit of harmony together for a definite purpose. Without this harmony your alliance will eventually fail. After choosing your members, it is advantageous to bring the members into the decision making process of determining your goals. This will give them a deeper connectedness and aid in the spirit of harmony.

Choosing Your Members

Now determine the first person you choose to work with. This must be done carefully. Do not choose one simply because you like them.

The number of members in your Master Mind alliance will depend upon your needs. After choosing the first person, then you two must agree on the third person. You do not just choose a third person by yourself, without reaching an agreement with your first chosen member. Once you both agree, you then invite the third person into your alliance. [In some cases this could be the basis for creating a band]. Then when choosing the fourth person it's imperative that you three agree on this person as well. This process guarantees, at least in the beginning, that all parties are willing and able to work together for a common cause. Also keep in mind that it doesn't matter if you are the smartest person in the room. If your personality or your actions dictate indifference or discord you will not get very far in this spirit of harmony. You must develop a pleasing personality.

John Mellencamp (American musician, singer-songwriter, painter, actor and Grammy winner . . . who also, as of 2018, holds the record as the first solo artist to hit number one seven times on the Hot Mainstream Rock Tracks Chart) said this: "I can find plenty of talented musicians to play in my band. I'm looking for guys I can get along with, especially the twenty-two hours a day we're not on stage." These are the types of attributes you will not learn in a music school. In essence, his statement is more proof that your band or group, in reality, is a Master Mind alliance.

It is essential that you respect each other and are one hundred percent willing to work together in a spirit of harmony.

Yo Yo Ma made this bold statement: "You know you can have someone who's one of the very best at something, but if there's not that kind of chemistry and harmony, then collaborating is not going to amount to anything."

Once you have initially established your alliance, whether it is just you and your spouse or partner, or a dozen people, it is imperative that the group as a whole become and remains active. You must move forward together toward your end result, keeping your timetable and your common purpose foremost.

In naming this chapter "Power Of The Master Mind," Napoleon Hill was specific in his use of the word "Power." He states it is not a dictatorial power, however, it is a power we use to our benefit, that is attained by gathering and acquiring organized knowledge. He states there are three types of organized knowledge in which to draw from:

1. Infinite Intelligence. This is one of the most powerful sources of knowledge used by creative people. You've heard it said, "The entire song or idea came to me within a five minute period. I don't know where it came from." This is explained further in Chapter 5, Imagination.

2. Accumulated Experience. This includes all formal and specialized education. This would also be composed of music and art lessons. Here he also includes the knowledge found in our public libraries. Today we also have the use of the Internet. Here it should also be noted that just because you are able to read data in print on your computer, pad or phone, does not mean it is one hundred percent accurate. It's always best to verify what you read before assuming it a fact.

3. Experiment and Research. In the field of science and technology and every other walk of life, men and women, are gathering, classifying, and organizing, new facts daily. This is the source to turn to, when knowledge is not available through "Accumulated Experience." This also applies to groundbreaking innovations, and new thoughts and ideas. Most modern-day advances in how music and art are constructed, are often harnessed with the power of your "Creative Imagination."

Knowledge can be attained by any and all of these three sources. This is where the Power of the Master Mind becomes a significant benefit.

To impress upon your level of confidence, here is an example of one of the most powerful Master Mind alliances ever created. That would be the power of Mahatma Gandhi. Gandhi came into power by compelling over two hundred million followers to coordinate their minds and bodies in a cooperative effort in reaching a definite purpose. This was done without force, only through peaceful inspiration in a spirit of harmony. What Gandhi accomplished was nothing short of a miracle. This is the ultimate example of a true Master Mind alliance, which took place in the twentieth century.

Dr. Hill explains: "The list of the chief sources from which power may be attained is, as you have seen, headed by *Infinite Intelligence*. When two or more people coordinate in a spirit of harmony, and work toward a definite objective, they place themselves in position, through that alliance, to absorb power directly from the great universal storehouse of *Infinite Intelligence*. This is the greatest of all sources of power. It is the source to which the genius and every great leader turn (whether they are conscious of the fact or not). This is the greatest of all sources of power, especially surrounding the creative powers to be."

I will explain more in an upcoming chapter, the methods by which *Infinite Intelligence* may be most easily used and brought into your understanding.

Here is the time for a disclaimer, as Napoleon Hill stated, "This is not a course on religion. There are no principles in this entire book that I intend to be interpreted in anyway as religious practice. I intend neither to interfere nor inspire directly or indirectly with any of your religious beliefs." The sole purpose of this book is to help you attain that Plane of Success that lives inside your heart.

You, Your "Other" Self, And You

I want to be clear in helping you understand that there is a warehouse full of power that awaits you, in forming and using this Master Mind alliance principle. It is also important to understand the term of, "doing for yourself." Do not think you can form a Master Mind alliance and expect them to magically carry you to your Plane of Success. You must do your part within the alliance. Any personal obstacles you are facing today need to be addressed.

Have you taken the time to introduce yourself to your "other self?" Know your "other self"—the one who knows no limitations—and you can become "The Master of Your Fate, and The Captain of Your Soul." Your "other self" is that power within you that is yours. Once it has been swept clean of all negative mental attitudes, it will manifest in your mind. It thrives in a mind guided by *faith*. Your "other self" pays no heed to any form of negativity.

You hold the power within you, as an individual, to contact *Infinite Intelligence* for the solutions to any problems you have. Of course you can also use this power to help guide you in the future to achieve whatever you believe you can. Likewise, if there is some given situation in your life, that you cannot eliminate for any reason, you at least have the ability to change your mental attitude so that the situation does not grow and continue to irritate you. Your mental attitude is the one asset in which you have complete control. Regardless of the circumstances, nothing is more important than the way you react to the situation through your mental attitude.

You need to get to know and understand the "other" side of your personality, the side that knows no obstacles nor recognizes any defeat. Please plant and harvest a new closeness with the "other" you. The "other" you, who ignores all obstacles, criticism, fear and doubt, so that no matter what you are doing, you are aligned with someone who embraces your goals.

All of the advice and principles in this book in regard to getting others to help you in your desires, will prove to be far more beneficial when you first put it to use on yourself, and your "other" self.

Then as you read, stop to think. Stop to meditate. Eventually as you devour chapter by chapter you will have "aha" moments. As you start understanding the details of each chapter, this entire philosophy will start to be revealed right before your eyes. Every chapter you read, study, re-read, and absorb, brings you one step closer on your pathway to reaching your Plane of Success.

THE PROFOUND PERCEPTION

Any dominating idea, plan or purpose held in the conscious mind through repetition of thought and emotionalized by a burning desire for its realization, is taken over by the subconscious and acted upon through whatever natural and logical means may be available.

Chapter 9 QR Code Recap
The Power of The Master Mind   Video Duration 8:01 minutes

This QR Code excerpt was created from "Your Right To Be Rich" series Chappell Enterprises L.L.C. and The Napoleon Hill Foundation

www.naphill.org/tgtam/chapter-9/   Available at: yourrighttoberich.com

10
The Mystery of
Sex Transmutation

The Tenth Step Toward Reaching
Your Plane of Success

Webster defines transmutation in this way: to change or alter in form, appearance, or nature and especially to a higher form.

Just the mere theme of these two words "Sex Transmutation" is somewhat confusing. Napoleon Hill studied and recorded information and data from thousands he studied in the early 1900s.

He reported; "Sex desire is the most powerful of all human desires."

Straightforwardly, sex transmutation means switching or transferring sexual energy from the physical act of sex to thoughts of a different nature. These thoughts include increased keenness of your imagination, courage, willpower, persistence, and creative ability that could remain unknown to you at other times.

Sexual desire is so strong and powerful that men and women (usually men) will risk their careers, life and reputation to indulge in it. This has never been more apparent than with all of the media attention beginning around 2017.

So let's try to wrestle through all this confusion and explain in a simple, modern-day way, the Mystery of Sex Transmutation.

Very simply put: You are going to transfer desire. This world we live in is all about desire. Desire for happiness, desire for success, desire for health, desire for peace, desire for the perfect mate. And yes, the desire for sex and as explained, it is our most powerful desire. Once you find a way to harness this power and redirect its energy you can transform mediocrity into genius. The key, is to consciously and deliberately cultivate and use your imagination and intuition while in a *"heightened state of mind."* There is a direct link here between the finite mind of man and *Infinite Intelligence.* Now you might ask, how do I reach this *"heightened state of mind?"*

First of all, you must have an intense burning desire and be very enthusiastic about it. You want to liken this enthusiasm to the same emotion that is motivated by sex. You must get your mind excited so it reaches a high rate of vibration. An example might be when your passion and sexual energy is completely focused and consumed on the quest of a certain person. Let's say your mind is telling you that you must have this person. Think about it, when you are in this state of mind, you are functioning or operating at the most desirable or greatest possible level of efficiency, speed, productivity and accuracy. You might go to all extremes to garner the attention of this person. You put on your very best game to impress this person. Simply put, your mind is hitting on all eight cylinders. The same element of excitement happens when you transmute that passion and energy into being more creative in your art.

OK, now you need a practical way to go about this. Here I will give you an example of how to use this power to access that part of your mind, we call genius. One way is to stimulate your mind by thinking about a past, current or future fantasy surrounding genuine love and passionate sex. Submerge your mind in these thoughts.

Imagine and feel in your imagination the excitement of this particular encounter. Notice how this exercise diverts your mind from your current challenges and concerns. This frees your mind to travel into the world of fantasy, leaving the challenges of life behind. In this expanded state of consciousness, you have access to sources of knowledge that you would not otherwise have, if, you were obsessing in everyday thinking such as worry and problems.

When using your emotion of sex to stimulate your mind to draw on *Infinite Intelligence*, you should be expecting insights of a new exciting nature. Not just previous thoughts re-arranged, however, brand new thoughts that just seem to pop into your mind and you have no idea whether or not they will work for you. This is the intriguing part in reaching this expanded consciousness. These new thoughts of course belong to you and only you.

This entire mind set of sex transmutation opens new doors of opportunity to you and your field of endeavor. In this world of fantasy, open up your mind to new exciting ideas, new thought patterns of creation, higher goals, or any impulse of thoughts that lead you to improving the momentum in reaching your Plane of Success.

Now that you have at least one practical way to transmute your sexual energy, let's take a closer look at how someone's personal magnetism is an expression of this energy:

1. **The Handshake.** The touch of the hand indicates instantly the presence of magnetism, or the lack of it.

2. **The Tone of Voice.** Magnetism or sex energy is the factor with which the voice may be colored, or made musical or charming.

3. **Posture and Carriage of the Body.** Highly sexed people move briskly, and with grace and ease.

4. The Vibrations of Thought. Highly sexed people mix the emotion of sex with their thoughts, or may do so at will, and in that way, may influence those around them.

5. Body Adornment. People who are highly sexed are usually very careful about their personal appearance. They usually select clothing of a style becoming to their personality, physique, complexion, etc.

Another simple example of how to use sex transmutation, comes from a start-up CEO. He said when he first started his business, he would take customer complaint calls. If the caller was a female, he would then imagine her being very attractive. He said upon doing this, his demeanor, excitement, understanding, and his willingness to help her, completely skyrocketed. Using this example you could, for all intent and purpose, picture the object of your sexual desire just behind your goal or challenge.

Let's say your goal is to run a marathon. You could picture the object of your sexual desire, waiting for you just across the finish line, wearing a bright red top, and a huge winning smile. By using this technique, I believe it creates a bond between your goal and your sexual desire which makes them inseparable. Understanding that sex is the strongest of the emotions, puts your goal on a higher playing field.

The Power Of Magnetism

Have you ever been to a party and you were suddenly drawn to a person telling a story? This interest was not due to the subject of their story, the attraction was due to their personal charisma. Did it seem as though for a brief moment, that they were the only person in the room? Did you feel like you needed to get within earshot just to hear what their voice sounded like? This was due to their magnetic charm or appeal, also considered charisma. Some profess charisma is a divine gift. You can practice certain skills that will enhance your personal magnetism. By enhancing your magnetic personality, you also enhance your ability in reaching your Plane of Success, at a more rapid rate.

Your most powerful personality traits are those that cannot be taken away by anything or anyone. Only you can give them away by sharing them. The more you share, the more you will have. It has been said, love is one of the things we give away, however, at the same time keep. It has been said, the more you give away, the more you will have.

If you doubt any of this, please try this. Give a smile to everyone you meet. Ninety-percent will respond with the same, or at least act accordingly. Share a kind word, or a pleasant response. Give appreciation with warmth from your heart. Give cheer, encouragement, hope, honor, credit and applause. Share good thoughts and love with your fellow man.

When you experiment with giving of yourself in these ways, you will also start to grasp one of life's most difficult virtues. You will learn how to bring about desirable and gratifying actions within yourself. When you share these traits with others, they will begin to multiply and grow. This is also in direct context to practicing your skills on developing a pleasing personality.

Here is a list of twenty-one suggestions that Napoleon Hill believes are important in assisting you in achieving and growing your magnetic personality.

1. **Good showmanship.** Understand and apply the art of catering to the masses.
2. **Harmony within self.** Be in control of your own mind.
3. **Definiteness of purpose.** Be definite in developing relationships of harmony with others.
4. **Appropriateness of clothing.** First impressions are lasting.
5. **Posture and carriage of your body.** Alertness in posture indicates alertness of the brain.

6. **Voice.** The tone, volume, pitch, and emotional coloring of your voice are important factors of a pleasing personality.
7. **Sincerity of purpose.** Builds confidence of others
8. **Choice of language.** Avoid slang and profanity.
9. **Poise.** Poise comes with self-confidence and self-control.
10. **A keen sense of humor.** One of the most essential qualities.
11. **Unselfishness.** No one is attracted to a selfish person.
12. **Facial expression.** It shows your moods and thoughts.
13. **Positive thoughts.** Vibrations of thoughts are picked up by other people; therefore maintain pleasing thoughts.
14. **Enthusiasm.** Essential in all forms of salesmanship and leadership.
15. **A sound body.** Poor health does not attract people.
16. **Imagination.** Alertness of your imagination is essential.
17. **Tact.** Lack of tact is usually expressed through loose conversation and boldness of expression.
18. **Versatility.** General knowledge of the important subjects of current interest and deeper problems of life.
19. **The art of being a good listener.** Listen attentively, do not break in and take the conversation away from others.
20. **The art of forceful speech.** Have something to say that is worth listening to and say it with all the enthusiasm at your command.
21. **Personal magnetism.** Controlled sex energy. Major asset of every great leader and every successful person.

I would suggest reviewing those twenty-one proposals for achieving a Magnetic Personality. Read again those you feel are the most important, and more so, those that you feel require the most attention. It does no good to merely read the list. Stop and ponder and consider how you can grow your personal charisma.

Just How Powerful Is Sex

The emotion of sex is an "irresistible force," which there can be no such opposition as an "immovable body." When driven by this emotion of sex, men and women, become gifted with a super power for action. If you can wrap your mind around this and understand this truth, then you will come to understand the significance of the statement that sex transmutation contains one of the secrets of the creative process.

To give you an example of this power or should I say, "minus this power," we only need to look at a dog or cat that's been spayed or neutered, or a bull that's been castrated. They become quite resigned, meek and mellow. Whether man, woman or beast, sexual alteration removes the natural fight, the driving force within.

The Ten Catalysts That Stimulate The Human Mind

Dr. Hill gave us ten stimuli in which your mind responds impulsively. Through these ten eye-openers, your mind may become "keyed up" to high rates of vibration such as, enthusiasm, intense desire, and creative imagination, to name a few. Here are ten catalysts in which he states your mind will respond to most freely:

1. The desire for sexual expression
2. Love
3. A burning desire for fame, power or financial gain, money.
4. Music
5. Friendship between either those of the same sex or those of opposite sex.
6. A Master Mind alliance based upon the harmony of two or more people who ally themselves for spiritual or temporal advancement.

7. Mutual suffering, such as that experienced by people who are persecuted.
8. Autosuggestion
9. Fear
10. Narcotics and alcohol

As you can see from this list, eight of these stimuli are of a positive nature and two are negative and destructive. He gives us this list for the purpose of enabling you to make a comparison of the major sources of mind stimulation. Topping the list of all mind stimuli is the emotion of sex. This appearing at the forefront of his list is the stimuli, which most effectively "steps up" the mind, and starts turning the wheels of physical **Action**.

Your Sleeping Genius

Obviously not a genius, a man once said, "A genius is a man who wears long untidy hair, eats food, lives alone, and serves as a target for joke makers." Dr. Hill gives a much better, understandable and realistic definition when he stated, "A genius is a man or woman who has discovered how to increase the intensity of thought, to the point where they can freely communicate with sources of knowledge not available through the ordinary rate of thought."

You might be asking now, "How on earth can a person communicate with sources of knowledge which are available only to geniuses? What and how am I able to reach and use these sources?"

Any person who possesses and displays normal mental capacity can develop genius ability. The public at large has labeled only certain types as genius. These labeled geniuses, in reality, do not have any powers you do not possess. After extensive examination of the lives of so-called geniuses, it was found that they are invariably people who are consciously and subconsciously following certain basic principles that are responsible for their plausible powers. The first and foremost principle used by genius is that of a Definite Major Purpose. A genius understands what he or she wants from life. Geniuses are busy, always moving toward their desires. Another major attribute and possibly the most important attribute used by genius, is a Positive Mental Attitude. It is impossible to reach genius capacity without constantly maintaining a Positive Mental Attitude.

As you read and digest the following chapters, more principles will unfold before you, and your understanding of how to awaken your sleeping genius shall be revealed.

THE PROFOUND PERCEPTION

Any dominating idea, plan or purpose held in the conscious mind through repetition of thought and emotionalized by a burning desire for its realization, is taken over by the subconscious and acted upon through whatever natural and logical means may be available.

The Sixth Sense

Science Magazine reported in April 2016, that human beings have magnetic receptors. This can help explain the science behind the ever-famous term "The Sixth Sense." It has been long known and discussed in great detail. This "Sixth Sense" is creative imagination. The use of this creative imagination is very rarely used by the majority of people; if at all, it is usually discovered by accident. Those who use this facility of the mind consciously, could be considered genius. This faculty of creative imagination is the direct link between the finite mind of man and *Infinite Intelligence*. All inventions and discoveries of basic or new principles take place through the faculty of creative imagination. The

Sixth Sense is such an important topic and valuable asset to understand, that it has an entire dedicated chapter ahead!

Do You Ever Have Hunches?

If so, where do they come from? In Napoleon Hill's years of research he came up with four explanations. He states, "When ideas or concepts flash into one's mind, through what is popularly called a 'hunch,' they come from one or more of these sources."

1. Infinite Intelligence.
2. One's subconscious mind, wherein is stored every sense impression and thought impulse which ever reached the brain through any of the five senses.
3. From the mind of some other person who has just released the thought, or picture of the idea or concept, through conscious thought.
4. From the other person's subconscious storehouse.

As you now know, your brain is both a receiving and a broadcasting station for vibrations of thought. By using your magnetic power of enthusiasm, it is possible to "step up" these vibrations in your mind. This is especially true when your enthusiasm is based on one of the four major emotions of love, hate, fear and sex. You must exercise self-discipline over these emotions as they have the ability to affect your enthusiasm and your brain in such a way, that they can make you or break you.

I keep mentioning the fact that you possess the ability, to "step up" the vibrations of your mind. In doing this, you are in effect, lifting your mind above the origin of ordinary thought. By reaching this level of mental capacity, it will permit you to envision a radius, not thought of before and not available on the lower level. The lower level is what we use when dealing with daily challenges in our personal and business routine. This higher level of thought, used with any of the mind stimuli, can be compared to ascending in an airplane. Here you reach a height where you may see over and beyond the horizon. Realizing also, while on this higher level of thought, you are no longer hampered by the concerns of attaining the three basic necessities of food, clothing and shelter. As your mind functions from this higher level of thought, your day-to-day routine is removed, which allows you to raise the physical limitations of your vision, just as you would as you rise in the airplane. You are able to see beyond the horizon into new territories.

While on this higher level of thought, the creative faculty of your mind is given the freedom to soar, search and reach. In other words, your mind has been cleared for the grand entry of your Sixth Sense. Your mind becomes open, making it available to thoughts and ideas you would not normally be aware of and/or use. Your Sixth Sense is what will set you apart from an ordinary person to genius. Use this power. It takes Practice, Practice, Practice.

Practice, Practice, Practice— Again Create, Create, Create

Many great writers, poets, artists and musicians attained greatness by consciously listening to that "one still small voice," the one who speaks to them from the inside, through creative imagination. The more use you give your creative imagination, or this creative plane of thought, the more wide-awake, energetic and dynamic it will become. By conscious usage it will become more receptive to factors originating outside of your subconscious mind.

Here I quote two noteworthy groundbreaking people from the early 1900s, in two very different areas of expertise. The first a prominent politician: "I close my eyes at the end of every speech, because then I speak through ideas which come to me from within." The second from a highly successful business leader: When asked why he closed his eyes two or three minutes before making a major decision he said, "With my eyes closed, I am able to draw upon a source of superior intelligence."

Both these prominent leaders were aware of the power in using this skill drawn from their creative imagination.

Creative Workshop

It doesn't matter if you're a poet, a writer, an artist or a musician, tapping into the creative side of your mind is a necessity. Any practice or technique that works for you can become of major importance, especially if you are stuck and can't seem to get over a certain hump. Here is a two-step technique, which has been beneficial to some:

1. Stimulate your mind so that it functions on a higher than average plane of thought, by using one or more of the eight positive mind stimulants, or another type that works for you.
2. Concentrate on what you have thus far, then use your creative imagination to try and picture exactly how you see your work once complete. Hold this thought or picture in your mind until your subconscious mind is in control of your thoughts. Now relax by clearing your mind of all thought and let your subconscious, your Sixth Sense, your creative imagination, bring you flashes of inspiration.

By using this technique, sometimes the results can be immediate. Sometimes it's even possible to get negative results. Other times it can take days or weeks. This is all part of developing this inner strength of the Sixth Sense or creative faculty. Again, the more you Practice, Practice, Practice, the more in tune you become.

The Sexual Drive To Success

Just the mere nature and subject of sex, sexual gratification, sexual desire, wants and sexual energy is uncomfortable and frightening to many. Many have been raised with the notion, that it's a taboo subject for discussion. Many have been taught it's a private matter surrounded by mystery and dark silence.

You have been learning that it's just the opposite. Being the most powerful of all emotions, how can we ignore it? Napoleon Hill cautioned us by saying, "The emotion of sex is a virtue '*only*,' when used intelligently, and with discrimination. It may be misused, and often is, to such extent that it debases, instead of enriches, both body and mind."

You don't have to look far to see sexual misuse and misconduct. Between the media, movies and everyday life, sexual misconduct has displayed catastrophic and destructive results. Dr. Hill also explained, "Love is spiritual, while just pure sex is biological. Love is without question, life's greatest experience. It brings one into communication with *Infinite Intelligence*. When mixed with the emotions of romance and sex, it may lead one far up the ladder of creative effort. The emotions of love, sex, and romance, are sides of the eternal triangle of achievement—building genius. Nature creates genius through no other force."

Sexual energy can drive the boat or sink the boat depending upon how it is guided. Let's take a glance at Madonna for example. Madonna is not only a talented musician, philanthropist and hero among some women, she is also known for her sexual presence as well as reinventing herself over and over to fit the current market. She is a perfect example of one who understands how to harness her sexual energy for creative purposes, and how to captivate audiences worldwide.

The Power Of The Spouse

You've heard it time and time again, "Behind every good man, there is a good woman" and "Behind every good woman is a good man" or today we have "Behind every good partner is another good partner."

This is as true today as it has been since the beginning of recorded history. A woman has the power to make a man or break a man. Likewise a man or mate holds this same power. It's been said, "Man's greatest motivating force is his desire to please woman." It can also be said, "A man or woman's motivating force is his or her desire to please their mate."

In today's world we have nearly as many career women bringing home the major income, as men. In prehistoric times, before the dawn of civilization, the hunter brought home great trophies so he might appear great in the eyes of woman. Man's nature has not changed that much. Today he or she brings home the income to feed, clothe and shelter their loved ones. Nothing has changed other than the method of pleasing and in some cases the woman is in the position of power and success. Men who become successful in any field of expertise, as a rule, actually strive for this success to please women. The same can be said of women. They strive to please their men, families, and show the world what they can accomplish. In some cases if you remove the man or woman from someone's lives, their spirit is broken and therefore their inherent drive is gone. They then must find another reason to forge ahead. What is usually the first thing they look for? You guessed it, another mate. Now you can see how this inherent desire to please your partner gives the partner, the power to make or break the other.

In most cases the person of power in the marriage or relationship will not want to admit or even recognize the worth of the power their partner holds. This is due to their nature, to be recognized as the stronger of the two. It is also understood, the intelligent mate recognizes this trait in their spouse and very wisely chooses not to make an issue of it. It's the old adage, "We know who's in charge here, and there's no need to show them."

Please do not deny yourself this truth and fact of life, for it alone has probably brought more men and women to the forefront of their respected fields and has helped more men and women reach their Plane of Success.

Chapter 10 QR Code Recap

The Mystery of Sex Transmutation   Video Duration 1:08 minutes

This QR Code excerpt was created from "Your Right To Be Rich" series Chappell Enterprises L.L.C. and The Napoleon Hill Foundation

www.naphill.org/tgtam/chapter-10/   Available at: yourrighttoberich.com

---

11
The Subconscious Mind

THE CONNECTING LINK

The Eleventh Step Toward Reaching Your Plane of Success

"Men often become what they believe themselves to be. If I believe I cannot do something, it makes me incapable of doing it. But when I believe I can, then I acquire the ability to do it even if I didn't have it in the beginning."

—MAHATMA GANDHI

She said, "Son, you can do anything you set your mind to." I must have heard my grandmother say that a thousand times before one day asking her, "What does that mean?" She said, "If you put your mind to it and believe it, then it will be." Today it sounds to me as if she was borrowing Napoleon Hill's famous words, "What the mind of man can conceive and believe it can achieve." It's that magic word *"believe,"* which gives this proclamation its validity. If we were to exclude the word *"believe,"* it would be of little or no use to us. Not only my grandmother and Napoleon Hill understood this principle, there are literally thousands upon thousands who understand it and *"believe"* it as fact. My question is, when we repeat our mission statements, who are we talking to?

Again my goal in *Think and Grow Through Art and Music* is to guide you to become a better or professional musician and artist. Please know that, I believe I can accomplish this goal and I will let nothing stop me. I started writing this book and interviewing artists in the 1990s. This is my definite purpose in life and therefore, I demand of myself persistent and continuous **Action** toward its attainment and I will let nothing stop me.

Does this sound familiar? It should by now. Of course there's more to it, however, I share it with you to make a point. Who am I talking to? Every morning, every night, upon retiring and several times throughout the day, I would repeat my mission statement.

Sometimes I repeat it aloud while looking at myself in the mirror. These are the times I can become animated by using one or more of the positive emotions. But, who am I talking to? Why of course, I'm sending vibrations to my own subconscious mind. Mixed with *faith* and emotion, these vibrations reach my subconscious and set me into motion. Motion that cannot be stopped, re-routed, misguided or criticized. My subconscious mind unfolds and lays out a daily path for me to follow. As I'm creating my everyday life experiences I grow to realize just how important it is to discover "who" is doing the creating.

I recall a wonderful story told by Napoleon Hill. In his oratory, he spoke about reaching a successful agreement with his publisher, who was pressing him hard to come up with a title for his book. Napoleon declared that on this particular night, he stomped up and down the floor and yelled at himself saying, "OK 'sub,' I need a title and I need it by tomorrow morning! I demand of you to hand over a title." The next morning he called his publisher and said, "I've got it. I will call it, *Think And Grow Rich*."

Did you happen to notice who he was talking to? Why he even gave it a name—"Sub." Your "sub" is your magic power that sets you apart from others. Give it a name, become friends with it. It can take you places you never dreamed of (or maybe you did).

The subconscious mind may be reached through *faith* and given instructions as though it were a person or a complete entity unto itself. In the beginning, you might have easier success reaching your subconscious by talking to it as if it were another person who was capable of saying yes or no. Your job is to persuade *'ol' sub'* in your favor. The good news is that you are capable, and this is well within your power.

President Woodrow Wilson and His Subconscious Mind

Upon retiring, Woodrow Wilson followed the habit of writing out a clear statement of what he wished to accomplish the following day. He would read it aloud several times in a nightly mission statement. Often, he would awaken during the night or the following morning, with the complete solution in his mind. At other times, the desired answer never came.

In discussing it in an interview with Dr. Hill, President Wilson stated, "The state of mind in which I ask help from my subconscious seems to have much to do with the results. In times of great emergency, under the stress of intense emotion, the guidance I need comes quickly. If there is any doubt in my mind, I also find the result is generally negative. But, when my belief is so intense that I almost feel myself in possession of the answer to my problems, then the result is always positive."

Wilson was convinced that the subconscious mind is the gateway to the *Infinite Intelligence* and can be used effectively only through that mental attitude of complete belief, known as *faith*. When you harmonize your mind with that of the ether, you gain guidance, power, and revelation, not available to you by any other means. In this way, your subconscious mind can help you reach your Plane of Success.

A perfect example of the use of *Infinite Intelligence* comes from Thomas A. Edison. A machine that would record and reproduce the human voice and instrumental music was merely a hypothetical idea in his mind, until he applied some of the principles explained in this philosophy. Mr. Edison who was familiar with these principles, planted his idea of this machine, with a Definite Major Purpose, and then submitted his idea to his subconscious mind. His subconscious mind transmitted his idea into the massive storehouse of creative power that we call *Infinite Intelligence*. He believed that by feeding his subconscious mind, *Infinite Intelligence* would divulge instructions for creating this machine. Looks like he was right!

Here is another example of how talking to "sub" and/or being aware and calling it by a name, can bring about great success. Many great scientists, artists, singers, writers, inventors, and poets have understood the magic of using both the conscious and subconscious minds simultaneously.

On one occasion the great Italian operatic tenor, Enrico Caruso (1873–1921), was completely overcome by stage fright. He reported that his throat was paralyzed due to spasms that were caused by an intense fear that had overcome his being. This fear constricted his throat muscles. Perspiration poured down his face by the bucket loads. He was shaking with fear and trepidation, as he knew he was expected to set out on stage any moment. His mind was telling him he couldn't perform. He said, "They will laugh at me, I just can't go out there." He then took a deep breath, collected his thoughts, and calmed his runaway mind long enough to shout so that all who were back stage could hear and witness his panic attack. He shouted, " 'The Little Me' wants to strangle 'The Big Me' within." (Caruso referred to "The Little Me" as his conscious mind, and "The Big Me," as being his subconscious mind). He said, " 'Little Me,' get out of here, 'The Big Me' wants to sing." Here he was referring to the limitless power and wisdom of his subconscious mind. He then began to shout over and over, "Get out, get out, 'The Big Me' is going to sing." Remember he was shouting to "The Big Me" which was his subconscious mind. The longer and louder he shouted the more he was taking control over his fear. His subconscious mind responded by relaxing the imperative muscles in his throat. When his queue came, he strutted out on stage and delivered a compelling performance. Obviously even back in the 1800s, Caruso understood the two separate minds. He understood your subconscious mind reacts and responds to the nature of the thoughts you feed it.

When and if this ever happens to you, you can practice exactly what Caruso and Napoleon did. They both spoke loudly and affirmatively, with a deep sense of authority, directly to their subconscious mind. You can make demands of your subconscious mind in any way you see fit. You will need to tell it, "I am in control, you must obey me, you are subject to my command and you must do as I instruct." In other words you must talk to "sub," take control and believe the words you are speaking, and back these with the strength of the emotions of *faith* and *hope*. In every example this will guide you to overcome any and all fear. Remember, fear only exists in the brain. Isn't this a profound statement to understand? Fear only exists in the brain. Have Faith!

Your subconscious mind houses an entire field of consciousness. Every "impulse of thought" or "vibration of thought," that reaches the "conscious" mind through any of the five senses, is classified and recorded. Once recorded, you may draw on them and use them at your will. I liken it to the shelf in the public library system. Once written down, recorded, and placed on the shelf, you are able to go in and withdraw any and all information that has been placed there. Please remember, your mind is a much more complex piece of machinery compared to that library shelf. Are you aware that your mind is capable of filing sense impressions and flashing thoughts, as well? You might be wondering, what is a sense impression? Consider a sense impression as an impression that's recorded in your memory, such as the smell of fish frying, or another example is looking at a stove with a red-hot burner. Do you actually have to touch that burner to know it's hot? No, your sense of touch automatically tells you it's hot, do not touch. The same can be said with flashing thoughts. How could one ever log the approximate 50,000 thoughts we have per day, it would be impossible. Our mind is capable of carrying on all these activities simultaneously. You cannot file sense impressions and flashing thoughts on a bookshelf. This gives you just a small window into the complexity of our minds. (Both of them).

As I pointed out in the chapter on Autosuggestion, your subconscious mind cannot distinguish between positive input and negative input. It will not challenge or modify your purpose, regardless if it is good or evil. It will try to bring about whatever thoughts you focus on. Your conscious mind is the sole guardian of your subconscious mind. Neither good nor evil, positive or negative thoughts, can enter your subconscious without your approval. The only exception to this rule are the thoughts that seem to come from the unknown, by way of your Sixth Sense. All sense perceptions you receive are halted at the door by your conscious, thinking mind. The exact nature of these most recent thoughts are now available for you to scrutinize, then let pass or reject. Your conscious mind stands guard duty, either letting thoughts in or rejecting them, from reaching and taking seat in your subconscious mind. It's a known fact that positive and negative emotions cannot occupy your mind at the same time. For example, if you are constantly worried or living in fear of not making it, or "trying but not achieving," then those negative thoughts will dominate your mind. You must replace them with positive thoughts. Either positive or negative thoughts and emotions will eventually dominate your mind, therefore it's imperative, for you to distinguish between the two, and start the habit of always replacing the negative with the positive.

I think Sharon Lechter says it best in her monumental work, *Think and Grow Rich for Women.* "By creating *the habit* of rejecting negative emotions and thoughts and focusing only on positive emotions and thoughts, you will see positive transformation in your life. Before long, you will see that negative thoughts literally bounce off your positively charged conscious and subconscious mind. When the two minds are aligned you have gained control over your subconscious mind."

Please notice that I italicized her words—*the habit*. I want to warn you to not become discouraged, if at first you do not feel like you have control over your subconscious mind. Remember, that your subconscious mind may be voluntarily guided only *through habit,* and by understanding the directions and principles given to you in the chapter on Faith. Please be patient and be persistent, because chances are, you have not had time to completely master Faith up to this point. All skills are learned by habit or said another way, "Practice, Practice, Practice."

I now suggest going back right now, and re-reading your mission statement and the chapter on Autosuggestion. Should I repeat myself in saying, I believe in the power of repetition? Again, some of us only learn by repetition. By reviewing the chapter on Autosuggestion, it will help prepare your mind to accept and understand the upcoming principles in this chapter. Do It Now!

Dr. Hill tells us we cannot entirely control our subconscious mind. Not what you wanted to hear, right? That's ok, he states that you can voluntarily hand over to your subconscious any plan, desire, or purpose and it will be transformed into concrete form. There is plenty of evidence to support the belief that the subconscious mind is the connecting link between the finite mind of man and *Infinite Intelligence.*

Once you have accepted, as a reality, the existence of your subconscious mind, and understand its possibilities as a source and a method to reach your Plane of Success, you will then understand the full significance regarding the major role of your *burning desire.* You will also understand more fully why you were instructed to put in writing this definite burning desire. In reality, once you have accepted your subconscious as a fact, you will have a clearer understanding of the entire chapter on Desire. By reducing your *burning desire* to words on paper, not only does your brain see the words you write, your subconscious also sees them and begins work at once. You will also now be able to clearly see the importance and necessity of persistence in carrying out these instructions.

Knowing now and understanding that you do have a subconscious, wouldn't it only make sense that you have always had a subconscious mind? Just because you are now fully aware of it, does not mean it wasn't there before. In an earlier chapter, I used the example of waking up just before the alarm clock sounded. Have you ever arrived at a destination in your car and not remembered how you got there? In other words, your conscious mind was elsewhere and your "sub" drove you there. Your subconscious will function voluntarily with or without your effort or direction. It will not sit idle.

Let's see how this can have a major influence and affect your day-to-day thinking patterns. Let's say, a colleague walks by and casually says—"You'll never make it." Your brain and your subconscious heard those four words. Right here you have a choice. You can let those four words play over and over in your subconscious, however, by doing this you might say to yourself, "Gee, what if they are right? Maybe I don't have what it takes. Maybe they're right?" Can you see how your mind multiplies all thoughts? You can easily relate to how your mind can run away, and even exaggerate four little words into a monumental picture of failure.

Or you can stop right there, as soon as you realize those negative thoughts have reached deeper into your mind. You can replace those negative thoughts by reading your mission statement. Read it twice if necessary. Now your subconscious mind will go back to helping you attain your Plane of Success and not allow you to start on a downward spiral. It takes practice until it becomes an instinctive habit.

Once you achieve this skill, you will be in possession of the key that locks and unlocks the passageway to your subconscious mind. Now you have become the gatekeeper and you are in one hundred percent control of who and what goes into your subconscious mind. You have the power to open the door to let in the good and the positive and to keep it shut when the bad and negative come knocking.

Again Willie Nelson shares his wisdom; "Once you replace the negative thoughts with positive thoughts, you will start getting positive results."

The Blending Of Principles

Just as I mentioned the importance of going back to read your mission statement and the chapter on Autosuggestion, I also want you to understand that it will be much easier for you to reach your Plane of Success, by the constant blending of all of these success principles.

Dr. Hill explained it this way: "Everything man creates begins in the form of a thought impulse. We can create nothing that we do not first conceive in thought. Every accomplishment in life whether good or bad, first develops as a thought. Through the aid of *imagination*, thought impulses are assembled into plans." Your *imagination*, when under your control, may be used for your creative skills and for the creation of plans or purposes that help you reach your Plane of Success.

All thought impulses, intended to help you reach your Plane of Success that are voluntarily planted into your subconscious mind, must first pass through the *imagination*. They must then be mixed with *faith*. Then the "mixing" of your *faith* with a plan or purpose, that is intended for submission to the subconscious mind, may be done only through the *imagination*. Your *imagination* is a key element here due to the fact that you need to visualize yourself already reaching your Plane of Success. This visualization is brought to life, realized, and joyfully pictured in your *imagination*.

By understanding the substance and basis of the preceding paragraph you can easily see that you will need a blending and cooperative effort in applying these principles, for the voluntary use in affecting your subconscious mind.

The Power Of Emotion

B.B. King said one of his goals was to connect his guitar to human emotions. He thought if he could tap into us through or by our emotions, he could reach our souls.

When I ponder the power of emotion, a line from a John Lennon song always comes to mind: "One thing you can't hide is when you're crippled inside." How true this is. In most cases, our entire outside being is actually only a reflection of our emotions inside. This brings the entire "theory of emotion" into the limelight.

You've already learned and hopefully have come to understand, that the subconscious mind is much more susceptible to influence by impulses of thought when mixed and blended with feeling or emotion. Emotion backed by enthusiasm serves to impress your dominating thoughts or desires upon the subconscious mind, where they are speedily acted upon. Thoughts that originate in the "reasoning" portion of the mind, without feeling or emotion, have little or no effect on the subconscious mind. They are more or less just instantaneous thoughts, passing through the conscious mind without being acted upon. Understanding the power of emotions is essential in using your "sub" to its highest potential.

You will know by the state of your own mind, when the habit you are feeding your subconscious has taken hold or has become properly fixed. How? You will experience a continuous feeling of enthusiasm. You will also be guided by an unwavering *faith* in your ability to reach your Plane of Success. You shouldn't be surprised when your subconscious mind wakes you up in the middle of the night with an idea or a new plan that will help you reach your Plane of Success. At times, situations will develop that just seem to occur that will give you confidence and determination. On occasions, for some unknown reason, people will seem friendlier and more helpful to your cause. Your mind will also put you on sharp guard as to these surprisingly unexplained opportunities that just seem to pop up for your benefit. You will see the world and those around you differently, because you will have shuffled the entire tempo of vibration all to your benefit.

Dr. Hill gives us seven positive emotions and seven negative emotions to consider. Please note, the seven negative emotions voluntarily impregnate themselves into the thoughts leading to your subconscious mind. Likewise, you must impregnate the seven positive emotions through the principle of Autosuggestion, as you learned in an earlier chapter.

The Seven Major Positive Emotions
The Emotion of Desire
The Emotion of Faith
The Emotion of Love
The Emotion of Sex
The Emotion of Enthusiasm
The Emotion of Romance
The Emotion of Hope

Of course, there are many more positive emotions, however these are the most powerful. These are proven to be the most influential and meaningful emotions that are commonly used in creative effort. By constantly practicing these seven major positive emotions, this will open the door to make available any and all others as you determine your need for them.

The Seven Major Negative Emotions
(UNACCEPTABLE AND TO BE AVOIDED)

The Emotion of Fear

The Emotion of Jealousy

The Emotion of Hatred

The Emotion of Revenge

The Emotion of Greed

The Emotion of Superstition

The Emotion of Anger

South African International Human Behavior Specialist, Mavis Mazhura said, "Emotions can get in the way, or get you on your way. When you are able to direct your emotions in the direction you want, you will improve your performance towards your desired goal and success will follow."

As previously stated, "Positive and negative emotions cannot occupy the mind at the same time." One or the other will be in control at all times. To reach your Plane of Success more easily, you will want to consciously take control of your positive emotions to guarantee that they are in the driver's seat at all times. This is where you will again need to Practice, Practice, Practice. By continuous and conscientious practice, you will form the habit, so that eventually and automatically your mind will not permit negativity to enter. Just a single negative thought in your conscious mind is enough to destroy all opportunity of using this magic power from your subconscious mind. Only by continuously following these techniques, will you be able to acquire complete control of your magic power, your subconscious mind.

THE PROFOUND PERCEPTION

Any dominating idea, plan or purpose held in the conscious
mind through repetition of thought and emotionalized
by a burning desire for its realization, is taken over by
the subconscious and acted upon through whatever
natural and logical means may be available.

Chapter 11 QR Code Recap
The Subconscious Mind   Audio Only Duration 6:51 minutes

This QR Code excerpt was taken from
the "Think and Grow Rich" Audio series
Available at: www.nightingale.com

www.naphill.org/tgtam/chapter-11/

12
The Brain

The Twelfth Step Toward Reaching Your Plane of Success

Back in 1938, it was estimated there were from 10 billion to 14 billion nerve cells in the human cerebral cortex. That number alone is hard to comprehend. As of late, researchers discovered the number to be closer to 16.3 billion nerve cells. This compared to the 14 billion previously predicted might not look like much of a difference, however, we're talking about at least an additional 2 billion nerve cells available for our usage.

Dr. Alexander Graham Bell (1847–1922) was awarded the first U.S. patent for the telephone in 1876. Dr. Elmer Gates (1859–1923) was an American scientist and inventor. Both of these men understood that every human brain is both a broadcasting and a receiving station for the vibration of thought. The creative imagination, in which we studied in the chapter on Imagination, is the "receiving set," through which the energies of thought are picked up. The Subconscious Mind, which we studied in depth last chapter, is the sending station of the brain, through which vibrations of thought are broadcast.

I find it beneficial to tie this thought process together to make it as simple as possible.

How does one of our most valuable tools, which we learned about in the chapter on Autosuggestion, figure into this mental equation? We already understand that the subconscious mind is the sending station and the creative imagination is the receiving station of our mental broadcasting equipment. So how does Autosuggestion play in? Autosuggestion is the medium by which you may exercise and turn on your broadcasting station. As you are using the principle of Autosuggestion by reading your mission statement daily, you are giving orders to your subconscious mind. Then your subconscious has the task of solving or bringing about outlines and practical solutions to meet your demands.

Tangible Brain—Intangible Mind?

Webster states: *Tangible* is capable of being perceived especially by the sense of touch. Therefore, *Intangible* is something that cannot be perceived by any of the five senses. So is there a difference between the human brain and the human mind?

Although there is some controversy, most experts will agree the mind is invisible, yet it processes incoming data and intelligence, accessing long-term memory, creating short-term memory and using conscious attention. Now what exactly does this mean? In more elementary terms, your brain (the tangible part) is physical. Your brain controls and coordinates your movement. It organizes your thoughts. It is the command center for your nervous system and feelings. Your mind (the intangible part) is designed to absorb information, sort through the thought process and bring about understanding.

The Power Of The Intangible

Dr. Hill speaks of our "other self" being more powerful than the physical self we see when we look in the mirror. What could he mean by "more powerful?" Let's take a deeper look into this explanation of "intangible." We are all controlled by unseen, intangible forces. Mankind does not have the power to cope with, nor to control the intangible force wrapped up in the rolling waves of the ocean. Man lacks the aptitude to comprehend gravity itself. Gravity keeps earth suspended and set in the exact right place in space. It keeps all of mankind from falling off of our planet. Man without a doubt, lacks aptitude to control this great force of gravity. Another type of an intangible force, not often thought of would be a thunderstorm. Just as we are rendered helpless in the thunderstorm, we also find ourselves nearly just as helpless in the presence of the intangible force of electricity. Before I show you how this all relates to you, your mind, and reaching your Plane of Success, let's look at one more intangible force and intelligence that are buried deep within Mother Nature's soil. Here is an unseen force that provides us with every morsel of food we eat and every piece of clothing we wear.

You can now easily see that these unseen, intangible forces possess a great power. You recall learning, that by feeding intangible, unseen thoughts into your subconscious mind, it can and will bring about, what might seem like miracles in our lives. To receive what might seem like a miracle in your life, from an intangible source, alone, is a monumental power. After all, it does make sense that Our Maker provided us with billions of nerve cells, they all cannot be for the purpose of carrying out our physical day-to-day functions.

How Much, What and Why, Do We Think?

It is estimated that we talk to ourselves at the rate of ten-thousand words per minute. This is not physical talking with lip movement, but an outpouring of ideas and images about yourself and everything you come into contact with. Your brain is sort of like a recorder and therefore, it records everything that happens to you.

It has also been estimated that you can remember, in your lifetime, somewhere around twelve-trillion individual pieces of information. By gaining understanding of just how many thoughts you have per day and more importantly, what kind of thoughts you have, it can help you understand the importance of the ol' cliché, "You are what you think about, all day long." These are powerful words and by now, you can begin to see just how true they really are. *"You are what you think about, all day long."*

Scientists tell us we have an average of fifty-thousand thoughts per day. The National Science Foundation gives us an estimate of twelve-thousand to sixty-thousand thoughts per day, depending on your mind and your given activity. Now, what kind of thoughts are these? After probing deeper, scientists tell us ninety-five to ninety-eight percent of these thoughts are the same as the previous day. They also alert us to the fact that approximately eight percent of these thoughts are automatically of a negative nature. These automatic, day in and day out thoughts occur in our subconscious mind. Now you can understand more fully how important the role your subconscious mind plays in your everyday life. You can see the need to be in complete control of the thoughts entering and flowing from your subconscious.

Imagine Invisible Practice

What does this mean? How can you imagine the invisible? In this example you will use your imagination to visualize your paintbrush, your instrument, or your *"physical art-creating medium"* . . . in the invisible sense . . . meaning it is not physically in your hand, it's in your mind's eye!

Yo Yo Ma is a huge proponent of this method of practice. He stated, "Practicing is not only playing your instrument, either by yourself or rehearsing with others—it also includes 'imagining,' yourself practicing. It has been proven that your brain forms the same neural connections and muscle memory whether you are imagining the task or actually doing it." This has also been proven true with all forms of exercise. When attaching modules to read brain activity, it has shown the same set of muscles are activated when imagining an exercise as in physically performing it. This can be most helpful when traveling, for example on airplanes. Just close your eyes and practice.

Again, add emotion as you visualize. Add joy, add *faith* into your "invisible practice." You will be continuously treading closer and closer to your Plane of Success.

Telepathy

A chapter on the human brain would not be complete for our purposes without mentioning telepathy and its role in the successful application of the *Master Mind* principle.

Have you ever answered a question your spouse was about to propose before they even got two words out? Have you ever had the phone ring and said, "It's probably so and so." Or possibly, you were thinking of calling someone or sending a text and the next thing you know, they are calling or sending you a text? Have you ever said these words, "What a coincidence, I was just thinking about you?"

This is telepathy. We have all had these experiences at one time or another. As previously mentioned, every brain is a broadcasting station and a receiving station for vibrations of thought. The human brain produces pulses (waves) of electricity in several frequency ranges. This knowledge has been applied in the field of medicine since 1929 with the invention of the EEG (electroencephalograph). This piece of equipment is used for recording brain waves.

When your mind is so charged with your goal of reaching your Plane of Success, it will attract the physical elements of that purpose. Chances and circumstances to bring about this purpose will seem to come from everywhere. In some cases their origin will seem obvious and others rather mysterious.

Eons before the invention of the radio, messages were transmitted. You carry in your mind a property or characteristic that is much like a radio receiver and transmitter. To understand this principle you must understand how a radio functions. A radio transmitter changes the vibrations of music and speech into electrical impulses of a much higher frequency. By putting a powerful force of energy behind these electrical impulses they can be pushed through the air until they connect with the antenna of a receiving set. In the receiving set the process is just reversed. It picks up the radio waves or electrical impulses and transforms them into mechanical vibrations of audio frequency that our minds can accept and our ears can hear.

You have this same power and ability in your brain. By some process that no one really understands, except by this radio analogy, you too can send and receive thoughts in the air or ether. It is yet another law of nature that your mind has been inherently equipped with, for this process. You have the capacity to speed up the thoughts in your mind to a high frequency and emit them in nearly the same way that radio frequencies are broadcast. Your brain has the ability to also pick up thoughts from other minds and bring them to the conscious level of understanding.

A perfect example of this is with your Master Mind alliance. When the subconscious minds of the members of your Master Mind alliance become blended together into an individual mastermind power, a power is released that the individual members do not each possess. It's this blending of thoughts that bring about these new and most useful realizations.

Just as you subconsciously accept the vibrations emitted by those around you, at times you must put up your guard. As I have mentioned earlier, approximately eight percent of those thousands of thoughts passing through human minds each day, is of a negative nature. Therefore, you will have those around you who are releasing thoughts of poverty, lack of harmony, ill health, jealousy and even hatred. Here again is where your mission statement will reign superior. You must develop your own unique style to protect your mind from this negative influence. By keeping your mind on your goal, knowing what you want, keeping a positive mental attitude and constantly going back and re-reading your mission statement, you can safeguard and protect yourself from accepting these negative thoughts into your own consciousness.

Napoleon Hill gave us this example, that he and two of his closest associates accomplished together. He said they had discovered what they believed to be the ideal conditions under which the mind could be stimulated so that the Sixth Sense, (explained in the next chapter), could be made to function in a practical way. He described their process this way. "The procedure is very simple. We sit down at a conference table, clearly state the nature of the problem we have under consideration, and then begin discussing it. Each contributes whatever thoughts may occur. The strange thing about this method of mind stimulation, is that it places each participant in communication with unknown sources of knowledge definitely outside his own experience." If you understand the principle described in the chapter on The Master Mind, then of course you recognized its practical application here.

By tapping into this unknown source of power and knowledge, he speaks of how you can expand your own thinking and receive the wisdom from *Infinite Intelligence.*

The Brain and Personal Initiative

Personal Initiative can be defined as a behavior that results in an individual, taking an active, self-starting approach to attain goals and persisting in overcoming barriers and setbacks.

It has been said, "The brain of man develops only by usage through personal initiative. Not everyone may recognize the possibility or the probability of the following fact well known to psychologists . . . behind all expressions of personal initiative, is the Creator's plan to insure man's mental and spiritual growth through his own endeavors."

Do you move upon your own initiative? If you have failed to move upon your own initiative in the past, and now have begun to follow the instructions I've outlined, then it's most likely you are presently making headway in your life. When you read the above statement, begin to understand that the Creator planted a seed or kernel of desire within you. This seed or kernel is your Definite Major Purpose in life and is a divine gift.

It is up to you to tend to your seed by nurturing it—through your own personal initiative.

One reason so many fail to take personal initiative, is due to their quest for perfection. Some decide if they can't do something perfectly, then they will not try it at all. One major reason for this, is as you've already learned, the fear of criticism and or failure. When you develop a Positive Mental Attitude, you don't give up due to having previously failed or because others have failed at a similar quest. You can be motivated and receive hope from some of your past successful experiences. It's like a baby who is just beginning to walk. The baby is not criticized for falling after taking the first three or four steps. Just the opposite, the baby is praised for the progress. Give yourself credit for the progress you have previously made. Again, you cannot win if you do not play.

Not beginning, can be the end of the road. Failing to start the journey, because of some preconceived roadblock, is catastrophic. Just turn on the ignition and start where you are, with or without a clear path of the roadway and journey ahead.

It's like the adage: "The Creator gives every bird its food, however, He does not throw it in the nest." You must take personal initiative in the development and proper usage of your brain.

Judy Williamson stated the following in her landmark work, *Napoleon Hill's Magic of Music* (a must read). "By taking personal initiative, you explore various options until you find the perfect size and fit, that will enable you to plant, nurture, and grow the seed of desire that you were given at birth. Your identity and gift are one of a kind. You are totally unique. Accept this priceless gift, move forward by taking personal initiative, and grow your inner seed until you have grown and blossomed in *Infinite Intelligence's* greatest creations."

Has your seed begun to grow yet?

Zig Ziglar (1926–2012), American Author and Motivational Speaker, always touted; "You were born to be a Winner, you must plan to win, prepare to win and expect to win." I have always agreed with his statement, there is a winner, on some level, inside every human being, including you. In all the history of the world there has never been anyone else exactly like you, and in all infinity of future times, there will never be. You are a one of a kind, you are a very unique person. Victory truly is built into you, and you are a Winner.

To further increase your own feeling of significance, consider this monumental struggle you have already accomplished in your "life." Just think, there were tens of millions of sperm cells that were in the great race of life, to reach that one precious egg which contained a tiny nucleus. You were the winner. You were the one who made it. It was on this microscopic level in which you won life's most decisive race. You had the will, the desire to live. The sperms in the race were smaller in size than the point of a needle. If you actually wanted to see this with the human eye, you would need to magnify it thousands of times.

More of your magnificence is the fact that you carried 24 chromosomes with you in your race, so you could merge with the 24 chromosomes in the tiny nucleus of the egg. Then you, the fastest, the healthiest, the winner—united with the mother's egg to form one, tiny living cell—You! You truly were a winner even before your birth.

THE PROFOUND PERCEPTION

Any dominating idea, plan or purpose held in the conscious
mind through repetition of thought and emotionalized
by a burning desire for its realization, is taken over by
the subconscious and acted upon through whatever
natural and logical means may be available.

As mentioned above, he believed that by tapping into this source of knowledge it would aid in your ability to utilize your *Sixth Sense*, which is the topic of the next chapter.

Chapter 12 QR Code Recap
The Brain   Audio Only Duration 3:37 minutes

This QR Code excerpt was taken from
the "Think and Grow Rich" Audio series
Available at: www.nightingale.com

www.naphill.org/tgtam/chapter-12/

13
The Sixth Sense

THE DOOR TO THE TEMPLE OF WISDOM

The Thirteenth and Final Step Toward Reaching Your Plane of Success

We understand, and in most cases, even take for granted our basic five senses; smell, taste, hearing, sight, and touch. Now introducing, and attempting to explain, in such a way that you understand your unseen and most powerful—"Sixth Sense." Your Sixth Sense is your *subconscious mind*, also referred to as your *creative imagination*. Napoleon Hill called it "The Door To Your Temple of Wisdom." He explains how it connects you to *Infinite Intelligence* and becomes the "receiving set through which ideas, plans, and thoughts *flash* into the mind." These *flashes* are sometimes called hunches or inspirations. He also states a special requirement in order to utilize this "miracle like" asset. He says you may only fully engage your Sixth Sense after you master the first twelve principles of reaching your Plane of Success. The thirteenth principle is known as the Sixth Sense; through which *Infinite Intelligence* may and will communicate voluntarily, without any effort from, or demand, by you.

Infinite Intelligence is the purest energy in the universe. It's the total of all the energy in the universe contained within a single entity. This entity is able to exchange information and communicate with every aspect of itself at any time, therefore, it holds within itself all the knowledge of the entire universe, past, present, and future. By understanding the first twelve principles, it gives you a clearer understanding that we are all connected to *Infinite Intelligence*.

As Dr. Hill states, We can "communicate voluntarily, without any effort, or demands by ourselves," therefore we understand that we currently use, and have used our Sixth Sense in the past.

A few examples: Have you ever been introduced to someone and immediately knew you did not like this person or felt this person was an untrustworthy sort? Have you ever had a gut feeling to do or not to do something, only to follow your gut, then find out you did the right thing? Have you ever walked into a room and felt uneasy and knew something was wrong, again to find out you were correct?

Another example, let's say you suddenly stop yourself from stepping foot into a winding street. Then a truck curves around the corner, you slow your heart down and say thank you. Who are you talking to? One philosopher claims that your subconscious mind can analyze and process data in a fraction of a second, which would otherwise take your conscious mind much longer. Therefore, in the example of the truck, your subconscious could have heard the truck coming and also saw the street you were about to cross. It then notified you to stop immediately and after recovering from the shock you realize that your Sixth Sense just saved you, and you say thank you . . . you were in essence thanking your Sixth Sense, your subconscious mind, and *Infinite Intelligence* simultaneously.

After you have mastered the principles described in this book, you will be prepared to accept as truth, the following statement which might otherwise seem incredible to you. Through the aid of your Sixth Sense, you will be warned of impending dangers in time to avoid them, and notified of opportunities in time to embrace them. Isn't this a wonderful thought; "To be warned of impending danger in time to avoid and to be notified of opportunities in time to embrace them," what an incredible power to have on your side. He refers to this as your "guardian angel," who will open "The Doors To Your Temple of Wisdom" at just the right time.

Your Sixth Sense will bring your *burning desire* into organized plans. With the aid of your subconscious mind, you will then take these organized plans and systematically step-by-step transmute them to permanent, concrete, and material reality. After believing, and accepting without being skeptical, then through Practice, Practice, Practice, you will transform your knowledge into *understanding*. Your newly found *understanding* will be expedited when you finally believe, recognize, and practice tapping into your Sixth Sense. You will be directed and guided to reaching your Plane of Success by being lifted to a higher level of mental stimulation and understanding.

Is Your Sixth Sense A Miracle?

A miracle is defined as a surprising and welcome event that is not explicable by natural or scientific laws, and is therefore considered to be the work of a divine agency. Dr. Hill, nor myself, are believers in, nor are advocates of, miracles. "Miracle-like" . . . yes. Miracle . . . no. "Seemingly Miracle" . . . yes. Here is his reasoning. There is enough knowledge of nature to understand that nature *never deviates from her established laws*. Some of nature's laws are so incomprehensible that they seem like miracles. Your Sixth Sense comes as near to being a miracle as anything on this planet.

He states; "There is a power, or a First Cause, or an Intelligence, which permeates every atom of matter, and embraces every unit of energy, perceptible to man that this *Infinite Intelligence* converts acorns into oak trees, causes water to flow downhill in response to the law of gravity, follows night with day, and winter with summer, each maintaining its proper place in relationship to the other. This Intelligence may, through the principles of this philosophy, be induced to aid in transmuting desires into concrete or material form. Step-by-step, through the preceding chapters, you have been led to this last principle. If you have mastered each of the preceding twelve principles, you are now prepared to accept, *without being skeptical*, the stupendous claims made here. If you have not mastered the other principles, you must do so before you determine definitely, whether or not the claims made in this chapter are fact or fiction."

Let The Great Musicians and Artists Shape Your Life

I made brief mention of this earlier, however, its significance is worth repeating. In my interviews, I had so many who said, "Imitation in one way or another, is a great teacher." *Emulation* is another word that was also mentioned quite frequently. What exactly is *emulation*? One definition of *emulation* is: To match or surpass (a person of achievement) typically by imitation.

Bob Ross (1942–1995), the famed landscape painting teacher, creator of his TV show *The Joy of Painting*, and an inspiration to thousands said this: "I think there's an artist hidden in the bottom of every single one of us, and I'm going to show you how to bring that artist out, to put it on canvas. In doing this I first want you to pay attention and try to imitate exactly what I do." He stated, "While in Alaska, I learned by watching, then imitating, William Alexander's show. Eventually you will develop your own form, color-combinations, and create your own style that belongs to only you. That's what we artists do; copy someone else until we come into our own. In painting, you have unlimited powers. You have the ability to move mountains. You can bend rivers.

Go out on a limb that's where the fruit is. You can do anything you want. This is your world."

In his soothing voice and gentle demeanor he would encourage you to paint your very own *happy little trees*. He also would say, "There's nothing wrong with having a tree as a friend." An imitator at first, turned inspiratory to thousands later.

Napoleon Hill spoke of a time he was going through a "hero worship" phase in his life. He himself was trying to imitate those he most admired. He said he had discovered that the element of *faith*, with which he endeavored to imitate his idols, gave him great capacity to do so quite successfully.

I share his following story and details so you might see the importance of aiming high. Here is his reasoning and a profound explanation, which is very beneficial in your understanding of why he had this habit. He said he first started this imitation practice, so he might reshape his own personal character. He believed the next best thing to being truly great was to emulate the great as closely as possible, by feeling and acting like them, as closely as possible. (This could prove to be most beneficial in creating your art as well.)

He created what he called his "Invisible Counselors." He chose these nine men whose lives and life-works had been most impressive to him. While lying in bed, during his imaginary council meetings, he listed them by name and recalled their faces. They were, Emerson, Paine, Edison, Darwin, Lincoln, Burbank, Napoleon, Ford, and Carnegie. His council meeting went something like this. At night before going to sleep he would shut his eyes, then picture in his imagination (the work shop of the mind), this group of nine men seated at his table. He said, here he not only had the opportunity to sit among those who he considered heroes, but he also dominated the group by being its leader and chairman.

As with everything Dr. Hill practiced, he also had a definite purpose for this exercise. As I emphasized above, he was rebuilding his own character, so these nightly meetings would represent a composite of his "Imaginary Counselors." He said he realized he needed to overcome his handicap of being born into an environment of ignorance and superstition. This is why he deliberately assigned himself the task of voluntary re-birth through this method.

Unconsciously, most people find inspiration in our everyday lives and this exciting world we live in. Sometimes, especially in the beginning of many careers it comes from other artist's art. There's always a basic "Aha" moment where you have said, "I like that," "I want to paint or play like that." A reminder as to what singer/songwriter Rodney Crowell stated, "If you hear something or somebody you like, then say, I want to play like that or I want to sing like that. Then start where you are today, and practice that sound until you get it. From there you will develop your own personal style." It is completely normal to begin playing or painting as closely as you can to your inspiration. Again, just as Napoleon spoke of reshaping his character by imagining himself in the presence of his nine "Invisible Counselors," eventually your creative juices will bring you into your own cultivated style of genius.

Tapping Into Creativity

It is a fact, that we human beings do receive input and useful knowledge from sources other than our physical senses. Located someplace within our brain is an organ which receives vibrations of thought which accept "preconceived notions" or "hunches." These might also be referred to as flashes of insight, revelation or intuition.

Some people express contempt for these hunches. They might say, "Today I had one of the most ridiculous ideas I could ever imagine." If you dismiss your hunches as foolish ideas, it won't be long before they too dismiss you! Pay Attention! All hunches should be treated civilly and examined carefully, as they often convey either in whole or part, information of the utmost value to you. At times these hunches may encourage you to modify your plans or to move on to a new plan.

When you have one of these flashes or hunches that seem to come from nowhere, write it down immediately. Then with an open mind, examine it. It is as equally important to write down any hunches that come to you in the form of questions. Who knows, the answer could be the very next step of your journey? This could be *Infinite Intelligence* endeavoring to reach and influence the conscious section of your mind, thereby aiding you with the exact inspiration you need at the exact time you need it. You will observe that they usually appear in the form of an idea, plan, purpose or desire, that comes to your aid through your subconscious mind. When you feel this enthusiasm you should recognize that you have been given this inspiration and you must act upon it at once. These hunches often make their appearance many hours, days or weeks after the thought that inspires them has reached the reservoir of *Infinite Intelligence*. If you delay, the desire will fade and slip away and the intensity of your feelings will disappear.

Remember your mind is similar to, and acts like, an electro-magnet to attract you to the things upon which you keep your mind focused. You are in control of what you are sending to your subconscious mind. This is a deep, profound subject, which even the wisest seem to understand very little about. By doing this, you are influencing these great powers to elevate you closer to reaching your Plane of Success.

John Prine (1946–2020), American Country Folk Singer and one of the most influential Songwriters of his generation, gave this advice relating to the importance of writing down hunches: "There have been times in the middle of the night I have a hunch for a song, that seems to have come from the unknown, and I say to myself, jeez, I'll never forget that. I went back to sleep and when I woke up, it was gone. Then later I'll hear something on the radio and say, jeez, I think that was the song I forgot to write down, that was originally sent to me."

It's paramount to write down these flashes, these inspirations that might seem either unimportant at the time or you think are so important that you'll never forget them. Take note . . . or should I say take notes?

Dr. Hill's research led him to the conclusion, that our mind is more receptive and open to receiving these "preconceived notions" or "hunches," when it is stepped-up to faster vibrations, such as under the influence of extraordinary stimulation. Please note, I'm not talking about stimulation through drug use. An example would be any emergency in which your emotions are inflamed or challenged, causing a more rapid heartbeat than normal. Again, we can liken this to having a near auto accident and within a split matter of seconds our Sixth Sense comes to our aid and saves us.

We can liken this to what Taylor Swift said in regards to her song writing. She stated, "When the anxiety starts, my song writing usually starts." She states that her best writing comes when she is anxious or her emotions are on high. (Again what happens when emotions are high or anxiety sets in? As a rule your heart speeds up, thereby elevating you to a higher plane of thought). Taylor goes on to say when she wrote her first number one hit, Love Story, it was while in an anxious fit. She wrote it as she stormed to her bedroom because her parents wouldn't let her go out with some guy. She was seventeen at the time. Talk about the *seed of an equivalent benefit or greater.* She took her *adverse situation* and turned it into a number one song.

To use your Sixth Sense to aid in your creativity in art and music, please know it takes practice. It's not something you can turn off and on like a light switch. You must first apply the principles defined in this book. Then pay attention to the times and places you are, when your creative juices start to flow. Notice your surrounding and your state of mind. Use these times and places to your advantage.

In 2014, the Office of Naval Research, earmarked nearly four-million-dollars to explore the phenomena it calls "Premonition or Sixth Sense." I found it interesting that they placed less emphasis on trying to understand the "how and why," instead concentrating more on the "how to use," ability of this inherent skill. The Pentagon reported that this study was born of field reports from war zones. The initial interest developed when a 2006 incident in Iraq, prevented carnage from an IED (improvised explosive device). Reports like these often came from the war zone detailing that a Sixth Sense had alerted them to an impending attack or IED, and allowed them to respond to a novel situation, without consciously having time to scientifically analyze the situation. Fast forward ten years and now the Defense Department has accelerated practical applications of this concept, by teaching active duty marines to hone precognitive skills in order to preempt snipers, IED emplacers, and other irregular assault tactics. Here, the government has proven the existence of the Sixth Sense without a scientific explanation of how it actually works.

I do not include this chapter on the Sixth Sense from a physic or superstitious outlook. This chapter was included so you might have at your bequest a complete philosophy in which you can guide yourself in reaching your Plane of Success.

As Dr. Hill stated, "The starting point of all achievement is desire and a Definite Major Purpose. The finishing point of this philosophy leads to understanding—understanding of self, understanding of others, understanding the laws of nature, and the understanding of happiness. This sort of understanding comes to its fullest only through familiarity with, and the use of the principle of the Sixth Sense."

I would like to caution you. Do not make the mistake of assuming that just because you do not yet 100% fully understand the principles of this philosophy, that they are not sound. By having *faith* and following these instructions you will be adopting the methods used by some of the greatest men and women who ever lived. There is nothing written here that is beyond your reach. Any person who displays normal, mental capacity can carry out these instructions and make them work successfully for their own benefit.

Having completed this chapter, did you notice there were times when you felt lifted to a higher plane of mental stimulation? Do you recall how you weren't actually moving, you weren't going anywhere physically, you were only lifted mentally? Do you recall what you were reading that set off this stimulation?

If so, Dr. Hill says, "Splendid! Now come back to this chapter a month from now and re-read it. Then you will observe your mind soaring to even higher levels of stimulation. Repeat this from time to time and pay no attention to how much or how little you learn at the time. Eventually you will find yourself in possession of a power that will enable you to ignore discouragement, master fear, overcome procrastination, and draw freely upon your imagination (the workshop of your mind). You will have then, felt the touch of that unknown 'something' which has been the moving spirit of every truly great thinker, leader, artist, musician, writer, statesman and stateswoman."

By grasping this power, you will be able to ignore all opposition and temporary set backs, and persistently keep pushing forward, inching toward your Plane of Success.

Alas, by this point in studying this philosophy, your mind should begin to function like a perfectly oiled piece of equipment. You have acquired the art of controlling your thoughts, your mind, and your emotions into a powerful driving force, which will lead you to reaching your Plane of Success. By now your imagination has become vigilant in alerting you to any and all opportunities. Your subconscious mind should now have a clear picture of you reaching your goal. Therefore, it is functioning with such power as to give you a set of plans and ideas in which you need, to finally arrive at your Plane of Success. As new opportunities and hunches appear, you can now understand how to act upon them immediately in the spirit of *faith*. Every hunch will be like a blueprint leading you toward success. Because you are one-hundred-percent focused on your Definite Major Purpose, all challenges will just seem like another obstacle to easily get around.

Any type of defeat encountered, will become nothing more than a signal for greater and determined effort. By now you should understand that every adversity carries with it the seed of an equivalent benefit or greater.

Having surrounded yourself with your harmonious and trustworthy Master Mind alliance, you have the luxury of using their gifts, their talents, and their ideas to help you reach your Plane of Success.

THE PROFOUND PERCEPTION

Any dominating idea, plan or purpose held in the conscious mind through repetition of thought and emotionalized by a burning desire for its realization, is taken over by the subconscious and acted upon through whatever natural and logical means may be available.

Chapter 13 QR Code Recap

The Sixth Sense   Audio Only Duration 6:24 minutes

This QR Code excerpt was taken from the "Think and Grow Rich" Audio series Available at: www.nightingale.com

www.naphill.org/tgtam/chapter-13/

14
The Six Ghosts of Fear

Take inventory of yourself, as you read this closing chapter and find out how many of the "ghosts" are standing in your way.

You say you don't believe in "Ghosts?" That's good. Napoleon Hill referred to these fears as "Ghosts" because . . . *they only exist in your mind*. They are not physically real, however, if you give them merit and lodging in your mind, they might just as well be real.

Do you know of people or friends who possess an enormous amount of talent and skill, including even knowing what they need to do to become a successful artist, however, they just don't use it? What could be holding them back?

There have been volumes written on overcoming fear. This final chapter is included to help you overcome any self-limiting fears and beliefs you might harbor. We start by naming our three major enemies—indecision, doubt, and fear. By naming these enemies and understanding them, we can armor ourselves with the necessary ammunition to overcome them. The Sixth Sense will never function while these three negatives remain in your mind. Indecision, doubt, and fear, are very closely related.

Where one is found, the other two are close at hand.

When indecision and doubt merge, they become fear. This blending process can happen so slowly that you are unable to observe it or become aware of it, until it overcomes your level and feeling of confidence.

Before you can overcome any obstacle, you must understand the how and why it works. You must know how this obstacle is trying to block your path, and more importantly, how to conquer it. It lives to defeat you, however, you are much stronger, therefore you live to defeat it. Sometimes these fears remain deep within your subconscious mind, which means they can be difficult to locate and even more difficult to eliminate.

Let's take a closer look at the "Six Ghosts of Fear" Dr. Hill has analyzed from his years of research. Please understand these fears can only exist in your mind. They have no other place to live, they have no permanent home, and if any do exist, they are only temporary. You have already learned that you are in complete and total control of your mind, therefore what do you have to fear? You are in control of what you let in, and what you refuse to let in. As Franklin Roosevelt (1882–1945) said, "We have nothing to fear except fear itself."

The Six Basic Fears

The fear of Poverty
The fear of Criticism
The fear of Ill Health
The fear of Loss of Love of Someone
The fear of Old Age
The fear of Death

There are other fears of course, however, these are the major fears. Any others can usually be listed under one of these. Let's now take a closer look at each fear and how to neutralize and conquer each one individually. Once you look at what you fear and why, you can take action that will remove it from your mind, freeing you to continue on your path in reaching your Plane of Success.

The Fear Of Poverty

The Fear of Poverty, is without a doubt, the most destructive of the six basic fears. It is the most difficult to master. You've heard the term "living beyond your means," well even highly successful people sometimes spend more than they earn. This too can create a mindset revolving around the fear of poverty and set one up for future failure.

To understand poverty we must first understand its opposite, Riches. For our purpose we will use the broader sense of Riches, meaning financial, spiritual, mental, and health. Once again, the starting point to achieving any and all riches is *desire*. In chapter one, you received directions on how to guide your Desire to reach your Plane of Success.

In this chapter on Fear, you will receive directions for preparing your mind to make practical use of your desire. Upon completing this chapter you will be at the fork in the road. Hopefully, you will make a decision to follow the path to reach your Plane of Success. We know where the other path goes. The responsibility lies within your mind, your desire, your ability to overcome all challenges, and to master every skill learned in this book—then Practice, Practice, Practice. Your entire ability to reach your Plane of Success lies in one area . . . *Your Mind*. And once again, need I remind you, your mind is the one thing you have complete and total control over. You are the master.

UNDERSTANDING YOURSELF AND THE
SYMPTOMS OF THE FEAR OF POVERTY

Our goal here is for you to take an honest, personal assessment of your-self. You've heard it said, "Keep your friends close and your enemies closer." In its broadest sense . . . we must recognize our enemies. To understand our enemies and overcome them, we must know who and where they are, and what they look like, which would include identifying any disguise they might be wearing. Some of this emotion of fear can be so deeply seated and subtle, that you may go through your entire life burdened by its existence, however, never fully aware of its presence. What an unpleasant experience to go through life carrying one of your enemies with you everywhere you go, totally unbeknownst to you. Now is your time to confront this fear head on, by making an honest, in-depth assessment of any of the following symptoms you might possess.

SYMPTOMS OF THE FEAR OF POVERTY

Indifference. Lack of ambition, initiative, imagination, enthusiasm, and self-control. Accepting what life hands you.

Indecision. Letting others think and make your decisions. Continuing to "sit on the fence."

Doubt. Generally expressed by alibis and making excuses for your fail-ures.

Worry. Usually expressed by finding fault in others. Lack of poise and self-control regarding alcohol/drugs. A tendency to spend beyond one's income.

Over-caution. The habit of looking for the negative side of every circumstance. Continuous talk about failure rather than success.

Always wanting to wait for "the right time" instead of making "the right time now."

Procrastination. The habit of putting off until tomorrow what should be done today. This symptom is closely related to over-caution, doubt, and worry. Spending more time trying to figure out how to get out of doing something than simply doing it.

Do you suffer from any of these symptoms? Here are ten antidotes to combat the fear of poverty spelled out by Sharon Lechter in her monumental work, *Think and Grow Rich For Women*.

1. Set financial goals . . . ask a financial advisor for help.
2. Get a financial education. With more education you will have less fear.
3. Don't rely on someone else for your financial security, like a spouse or partner.
4. Spend less than you earn—it's really that simple!
5. Build an emergency fund.
6. Start investing—start small and build.
7. Pay attention and be engaged in your day-to-day money management, talk about it with your spouse or partner.
8. Keep an eye on your credit score and work to get it as high as possible.
9. Don't spend money to make yourself feel good.
10. Learn from your money mistakes.

By mastering these antidotes, and acknowledging that fear exists only in your mind, you will possess the skillset needed to easily conquer this fear of poverty.

This poem, written by Jessie B. Rittenhouse (1869–1948), pretty much sums up the concept of life handing you what you ask for.

My Wage
I bargained with Life for a penny
And Life would pay no more;
However, I begged at evening
When I counted my scanty store.

For Life is a just employer;
He gives you whatever you ask.
But once you have set the wages,
Why, you must bear the task.

I worked for a menial's hire
Only to learn dismayed
That any wage I had asked of Life,
Life would have willingly paid.

The Fear Of Criticism

The fear of criticism can diminish your power of imagination, your initiative, your individuality, and take away your self-reliance (confidence). I would like to point out one area where criticism does the most damage. Young children. Possibly at one time or another, some unknowing parent told their child they would never amount to anything, or they would probably end up in jail. In some cases the child believes their mom or dad and does just that. Please consider the alternative.

What if the parent repeatedly told the child that they would be a great writer, or a great artist, or had what it took to become a business leader, and that they would grow up to make a positive impact on this world?

Lyle Lovett, Texas born, American Singer-Songwriter, Actor, had this to say regarding parental influence; "I don't know where creativity comes from, but I think everybody has the ability to be creative. I think what's important about creativity, starts when you are very young, and how you are allowed to experience your imagination. The people, who bring us up and teach us, are fundamental in either encouraging creativity or discouraging creativity. My imagination was always encouraged." I can only hope you had the same encouragement and that you too, will pass on this same level of inspiritment to your children.

Let's now take another honest, personal assessment and see if you suffer from any of the symptoms of the Fear of Criticism.

SYMPTOMS OF THE FEAR OF CRITICISM

Self-Consciousness. Generally expressed through nervousness, timidity especially in meeting new people, awkward movement of the hands and limbs, or shifting of the eyes.

Lack of Poise. Expressed through lack of voice control, nervousness, poor posture, poor memory.

Personality. Lacking in firmness of decision, personal charm, and ability to express opinions definitely. Boasting. Imitating others. Agreeing with others without examining the facts. Being a yes person.

Inferiority Complex. The habit of expressing self-approval as a means of covering up a feeling of inferiority. Using big words to impress others. Boasting of imaginary achievements. Trying to be or act like someone you are not.

Extravagance. The habit of trying "to keep up with the Joneses"; spending beyond one's income.

Lack of Initiative. Failure to embrace opportunities, fear to express personal opinions, lack of confidence in one's own words, being evasive or deceitful in both words and deeds.

Lack of Ambition. Mental and physical laziness, lack of self-assertion, slowness in reaching decisions, easily influenced by others, unwillingness to accept the blame for mistakes.

As I previously pointed out, the fear of criticism can hold you back, slow you down, and possibly even try to detour your path in reaching your Plane of Success. I have two antidotes when overcome by this fear. First, read your mission statement, one, two, three times, if necessary. If you still need more direction just repeat, "I don't care what *"they say."* *"They"* are not me. *"They"* do not understand my path. I am in control of my thoughts and actions. I choose to ignore what *"they"* might say. No one can stop me.

Diana Ross of the successful Motown singing group, *The Supremes*, said, "Criticism, even when you try to ignore it, can hurt. I have cried over many articles written about me, but I move on and don't hold on to that."

I'm compelled to also include a quote from Eleanor Roosevelt who was First Lady of the United States from 1933–1945. "Do what you feel in your heart to be right—for you'll be criticized anyway. You'll be damned if you do, and damned if you don't."

The Fear Of ILL Health

The seed of the fear of ill health, sickness, and disease, is buried someplace in almost every human mind. Worry, fear, discouragement, stress, disappointment in love and business affairs, cause this seed to germinate and grow. If left to blossom on its own accord, it can completely demobilize the human body.

In today's world we have the media and the large pharmaceutical companies selling us on the idea of ill health and disease. They preach that any illness, including the common cold, is a deficiency of one of their prescribed drugs. In some cases when their patent expires, it becomes available over the counter, at a fraction of the previous cost.

We are continuously bombarded by the latest health craze or super-food or miracle vitamin. These companies understand people are motivated by fear. When they run their television, radio, magazine, podcasts, emails, direct mail, and in-person advertisements, the common day man might think, "With all this ill health in the world, surely something must be wrong with me. I wonder what it is?" And then some will start looking. We've all heard the stories about the co-workers who played a trick on their boss. All morning long co-workers would make statements to their boss such as, "Are you ok? You don't look well." or "Do you feel ok, you look pale." or "You don't look like yourself, are you ill?" Sure enough, in some cases, that afternoon the boss goes home sick. In some situations, they were sick the following day as well. This is how easily your mind is influenced, and the power it has over our bodies, especially when motivated by fear.

It has been recorded that approximately eight to ten percent of our population is preoccupied with disease to the point of hypochondria (imaginary illness). Experts advise us that the fear of disease, even where there is not the slightest cause or anything to substantiate the belief, will often produce the physical symptoms of the disease feared. You can now appreciate the strength and power of the human mind. It can build up and create, or it can destroy.

Naomi Judd (Country singer-songwriter) said, "Your body hears everything your mind says."

THE SYMPTOMS OF ILL HEALTH

Autosuggestion. Looking for, and expecting to find, the symptoms of all kinds of disease. Trying the latest fad and home remedies. The constant talk of illness, disease, operations, and accidents of those around you.

Hypochondria. The habit of talking about illness, concentrating the mind upon disease, and expecting it to appear. It is a medical term for imaginary disease. It is said to do as much damage, on occasion, as the disease you fear.

Lack of Exercise. Interferes with proper physical exercise.

Susceptibility. The Fear of Ill Health breaks down nature's body-resistance, and creates a favorable condition for any form of disease.

Self-coddling. Using imaginary illness to get sympathy and attention. The habit of feigning illness to cover up one's laziness.

Intemperance. The habit of using alcohol or drugs to "treat" pains, instead of looking for and eliminating the actual cause. It's the ol' saying, "A headache is a Darvon deficiency."

An antidote to combat the fear of ill health, could be as simple as repeatedly reciting Emile Coue's famous quote, "Every day in every way, I'm getting better and better." Another antidote would be to repeatedly recite, "Every day in every way, I'm getting stronger and healthier."

The Fear Of Loss Of Love

This is the most painful of the six basic fears. It brings more misery and devastation to one's mind and body than any other basic fear. When thoughts such as "I can't live without that person" enter the human mind, some will take it literally and resort to suicidal thoughts.

Research has shown that women are more susceptible to this fear than men. Research also explains this fact by saying women have learned, from experience, that some men are polygamous by nature.

SYMPTOMS OF THE FEAR OF LOSS OF LOVE

Jealousy. Being suspicious of friends and loved ones, without any reasonable evidence. General suspicion of everyone.

Fault-finding. Finding fault with friends, relatives, business associates and loved ones for no apparent reason.

Gambling. Gambling, stealing, cheating, and otherwise taking hazardous chances to provide money for loved ones, with the belief that love can be bought.

This emotional pain can feel far worse than physical pain. If one can muster the confidence to say, "It's their loss, more than mine," then the emotional pain can be somewhat diminished.

One of the best antidotes is to remember this quote by Napoleon Hill, it will help put the situation into perspective; "Every adversity comes with it, the seed of an equivalent benefit or greater." It's best to start looking for that seed as quickly as possible.

The Fear Of Old Age

There are many reasons people fear old age. In some cases it's not the fear of aging, but the fear of being alone, or even loss of certain capacities. In other cases you may have witnessed suffering and the inability to help one's self. There can be many factors that come into play.

SYMPTOMS OF THE FEAR OF OLD AGE

Slowing Down. Believing one's mental capacity is slipping, due to age.

Apologizing for being old. Speaking apologetically for "being old" rather than being grateful for achieving the age of wisdom and understanding.

Losing One's Confidence & Insight. The habit of extinguishing one's initiative, imagination, and self-reliance by falsely believing one's self too old to exercise these qualities.

Appearance in Dressing & Actions. Trying to act and dress like a much younger person.

An appropriate antidote here, is to look forward to the future regardless of age. Have a goal for age seventy-five? Have a goal for age eighty-five, ninety-five or one hundred? Striving toward goals, regardless of age, will continue to keep the fire lit and give you something to look forward to, rather than dwelling on how things used to be. Stay active, both physically and mentally.

The Fear Of Death

The end. Some become anxious when contemplating the end. Of course we all know what we've been taught. We either go up or down. In some cases it's the fear of the unknown. Napoleon Hill reminds us that men of science have turned the spotlight of truth upon the world. They have come to understand this entire world to be made up of two things, energy and matter. In physics, we have been taught that neither matter nor energy can be created or destroyed. He states; "Life is energy, if it is anything. If neither energy nor matter can be destroyed, then of course life cannot be destroyed. Life, like other forms of energy, may be passed through various processes of transition, or change, but it cannot be destroyed. Death is a mere transition."

SYMPTOMS OF THE FEAR OF DEATH

Contemplation. The habit of entertaining death and thinking about dying rather than making the most out of what one has left. This is generally due to a lack of purpose.

Causes. The most common causes of the fear of death are: ill health, poverty, lack of appropriate occupation, disappointment over love, insanity, and religious fanaticism.

"The greatest of all antidotes and remedies, for the fear of death is a *burning desire* for achievement, backed by useful service to others. A busy person seldom has time to think about dying. He or she finds life too thrilling to worry about death."

Worry

"Worry is a state of mind based upon fear. It works slowly, but persistently. It is insidious and subtle. Step-by-step it 'digs itself in' until it paralyzes one's reasoning faculty, destroys self-confidence and initiative. Worry is a form of sustained fear caused by indecision; therefore it is a state of mind that can be controlled."

Now this quote from Winston Churchill (British Writer and Prime Minister of Great Britain 1940–1945 and 1951–1955), "Worry is a thin stream of fear trickling through the mind. If encouraged, it cuts a channel into which all thoughts are drained."

There is a difference between worry and concern. A worried person sees worry as a problem, and a concerned person sees worry as a problem to solve. Worry can seem insurmountable or as a concern to merely break down and to find a practical solution.

As John Lennon profoundly and simply said, "There are no problems, only solutions."

Indecision will cause you to worry. If you lack the ability to make a decision, it opens the door to worry. Likewise, by reaching a decision and following a definite line of action, the door to worry remains closed.

All six of these basic fears become translated into worry, through indecision. It's best to make a decision today to incorporate a plan to overcome each one of these fears. Here are more examples of how to overcome your fears: Relieve yourself from the fear of death by reaching a decision to accept it as an inescapable part of life. Whip the fear of poverty by reaching a decision to accumulate wealth and success without worry. Reach a decision to never worry about what "they say" or what people might think of you by their criticism. Eliminate the fear of old age by reaching a decision to accept it and embrace the lifetime of wisdom, self-control and understanding. Free yourself of the fear of ill health by making a decision to forget all symptoms. Master the fear of loss of love by making the decision to love yourself and to be happy and if necessary, to get along without the love you desire.

Nothing which life has to offer is worth the price and the damage worry can bring about. Make the decision to never worry. By making this decision you will find peace of mind, poise and the serenity of thought which will bring you confidence and happiness.

Again I quote Dr. Hill: "You are the master of your own earthly destiny just as surely as you have the power to control your own thoughts. You may influence, direct, and eventually control your own environment, making your life what you want it to be—or, you may neglect to exercise the privilege which is yours, to make your life to order, thus casting yourself upon the broad sea of 'circumstance' where you will be tossed hither and yon, like a ship on the waves of the ocean."

By conquering all six ghosts of fear you are building a firm foundation with a designated corridor to reach your Plane of Success.

The Devil's Workshop The Seventh Basic Evil

In addition to the six basic fears, Dr. Hill also adds what he refers to as "The Seventh Basic Evil." He claims it constitutes a very fertile soil in which the seeds of failure take root easily and rapidly. It is so subtle that its presence goes unnoticed. He classifies this as *Evil* not *Fear*. "It

Is More Deeply Seated And More Fatal Than All The Six Basic Fears." He defines this evil as *Being Susceptible to Negative Influences.*

Negative Influences come from many sources. They can sneak into your subconscious without your awareness. Nearly everyday we encounter negative people casting negative remarks. In some cases just the fact that you hear negativity, might cast enough doubt on your desire to set up shop right there in your mind. It can be as deadly as poison. Over time, these outside *negative influences* may kill one's dreams at a very slow pace.

HOW TO COMBAT THIS SEVENTH BASIC EVIL

Again to combat an enemy you must first understand it. We all know negative people. As a rule they are complaining about something, everyday. They are very judgmental of others, they usually want you to join in their "pity-party" so they can feel better about themselves. Have you ever noticed how one negative thought connects itself to another, and another and another? These people have a habit of sucking all the life force right out of your body and zapping your energy, if you allow them. Usually by the time you realize it, it's too late. By this person or people casting their net of negativity, it affects your emotions. When your emotion is affected, then you actually feel the down-turn in your spirit. This is the time to put up your safeguards, and build a wall of immunity against negative influences in your own mind.

One of the most common problems people have is the habit of leaving their minds wide open so some stranger full of negativity can stroll right in and set up camp. In most cases your own two feet are the best defense you have, to defend yourself from negativity. It's easy to say, "Oh, I just remembered something I need to do." In reality, you are being honest . . . the something you need to do is get away from them. If you can't make a get-away then it's best to observe without absorbing. Then when they're done you might ask if they have a solution. Then make your get-away. Negativity is contagious. Negativity breeds negativity. Your own personal wall is important to protect yourself. Recognize and remember you have willpower. You have a definite aim. You have a powerful mission statement. Use it.

Constantly repeated throughout this entire book are the words, "You have absolute control over but one thing, and that is, your thoughts." Dr. Hill goes on to state, "This is the most significant and inspiring of all facts known to man. It reflects our divine nature. This divine prerogative is the sole means by which you may control your own destiny. If you fail to control your own mind, you may be sure you will control nothing else. *Your mind is your spiritual estate.* Protect and use it with the care to which divine royalty is entitled. You were given willpower for this purpose."

Your Plane Of Success

Although I don't know you, or know of you (yet), I feel an affinity just knowing you have read this far into this book. Through these pages, I feel as though we have met.

Please know that Napoleon Hill's principles have brought monumental success to scores of men and women all across our globe. I have adapted his principles to suit your needs in aspiring to become a professional musician and artist. These basic principles have brought great success into thousands of lives. My adapted principles when reinforced with his words (both written and spoken) will, without a doubt, not only guide you in reaching your Plane of Success, they will elevate you above and beyond, ultimately taking you to the very top. You will then be able to look back, smile, and confidently say, "I did it."

The only limitations you have are those that you set up in your own mind. You now possess a concrete philosophy of individual achievement. You have been provided a practical means by which to take, and keep possession of your own mind, and direct it toward harmony in human relationships. This will bring about happiness and peace of mind.

When you have assimilated this philosophy, you will most likely enjoy as good as or possibly a better understanding, than someone who graduates college with a Master of Arts degree. You will be in possession of an abundance of everyday useful knowledge, handed down from some of the most successful people this nation has ever produced. This group not only consists of artists, it also includes men and women from all walks of life.

It is now your responsibility to use this information wisely. The mere possession will take you absolutely nowhere, unless you use it by taking Action from right where you sit at this exact moment. Then you can say you are officially on your way to reaching and enjoying your Plane of Success.

Chapter 14 QR Code Recap
The Six Ghosts of Fear   Audio Only Duration 11:35 minutes

This QR Code excerpt was taken from
the "Think and Grow Rich" Audio series
Available at: www.nightingale.com

/www.naphill.org/tgtam/chapter-14/

Positive Mental Attitude

Congratulations for completing *Think and Grow Through Art and Music*. As a bonus, we have included this fifteenth QR Code. I believe that the ability to maintain a Positive Mental Attitude (PMA) heads the list of overall requirements in reaching your Plane of Success. In 1937, Napoleon Hill was the first to introduce the concept of PMA. In this Bonus video he lays out twenty instructions to help reinforce and maintain your Positive Mental Attitude, which in turn will make your journey easier and much more exciting. Denis Waitley said: "Virtually nothing on earth can stop a person with a Positive Mental Attitude who has his or her goals clearly in sight." I would add, "If you are going to have an attitude, then by golly make it *Positive*."

BONUS: Positive Mental Attitude

www.naphill.org/tgtam/chapter-15/

Video QR Code Duration 7:40 minutes

This QR Code excerpt was created from "Your Right To Be Rich" series Chappell Enterprises L.L.C. and The Napoleon Hill Foundation Available at: yourrighttoberich.com

Acknowledgments

The Spiritual Department

I would first and foremost like to express my gratitude to "The Spiritual Department." The glory goes to God, Our Creator, for giving me this phenomenal life filled with boundless opportunities and endless possibilities. I would be remiss not to also mention the inspiration available to all, and passed down, also in a spiritual nature . . . the ether, also referred to as Infinite Intelligence, and/or the Universal Library of Knowledge. This unseen power moved my pen across the paper at 4 and 5 a.m. on many a morning.

The Encouragement Department

Some of our most meaningful and powerful encouragement comes at a young age. I thank the woman who raised me, my Grandmother Bunny, for drilling these words in my head through repetition; "You can do anything you set your mind to." Many times, when I felt like giving up, I could hear her speaking those words in my mind's ears.

I also thank Mr. Andrew Carnegie who inspired the young lad Napoleon Hill, to write the first science of personal success. From these writings, not only have I been encouraged beyond belief, so have many thousands of others, who have improved their lives by applying his principles.

The friends and family department of encouragement could fill three chapters, so I'll make it brief.

Enduring gratitude I graciously bestow upon my darling wife Cindy-rae Faulkner, my daughters, Christian Michelle Penrose, Angela Rae Gosling and her husband Mark, sons James Kennedy Faulkner, Jeffrey Wayne Faulkner and his wife Susan, son, Chad Justin Gray and his wife Laura. I also appreciate all support that I received from my brothers, sisters, cousins, aunts, uncles and the entire extended family of love.

I have an all-important amount of appreciation for the greatest mother-in-law on earth, Mrs. Carmen Marquez . . . for all she does by spreading her love. I thank her for always being herself, and for bearing her daughter.

Nudge gratitude goes to five friends with five words—I have five friends whose five words are still echoing in my mental chamber: "How's the book coming along?" Thank you for your constant inquiries. Barbara Ann Bailey, Bill "Gino" Fernandes, Jeffrey D. "Jackson" Mandt, Elizabeth Ellen Morley Matthews, and Steven P. Sybesma.

Appreciated and loved all the nudges . . . all the time.

Contributing Mentor Department

This department is broken down into two separate departments.

A. The Les Paul Guidance Department

B. The Contributing Artist Input Department

A. THE LES PAUL GUIDANCE DEPARTMENT

First, I must thank Rusty Paul and Lou Pallo. These two gentlemen gave me the confidence and the "how to," "where to," and "when to," approach Mr. Les Paul. First, Rusty would say, "Just keep on him." Him, meaning his dad, Les Paul. Rusty would also inform me as to who would most likely be joining Les on stage on any given night, so I could gather my thoughts beforehand. In the beginning, when I felt like giving up, Lou Pallo would first flash his winning smile, then when the time was right, after shows, he'd basically take me by the hand to wiggle my way into Les' space and life. They were both very kind and considerate of my quest. Due to their initial "how to's," the next four years were a breeze. Lou is known as "The Man of a Million Chords" and is also recognized for his unique style of singing, which is only surpassed by his genteel soul and spirit.

B. THE CONTRIBUTING ARTIST INPUT DEPARTMENT

Second, I thank all of the artists and musicians, who gave unselfishly of their time by sharing advice and making suggestions, eminently, Mr. Les Paul for sharing his wit and permitting me to be in the presence of such great artists. By conducting in person, and online interviews, I was able to acquire a better understanding of how artists think and accordingly reflect those thoughts into words, therefore helping my readers. The invaluable lessons in this book would not be possible if not for them.

"The Being There When I Needed Them" Contacts Department

A huge shout of appreciation goes to Lori Lousararian-Hakola, Vice President/Rogers and Cowan, Los Angeles, CA; Robert Norman at CAA, Creative Artists Agency, Los Angeles, CA; Paul Easton at Talent Ventures, Naples, FL, who for over forty years has been in the entertainment industry managing artists and producing music events, and Amy at Celebrity Service International, Hollywood, CA.

These four top notch individuals not only helped me with artist contact information, they also guided me with proper etiquette and phrasing so that I would receive a positive response. I would not have had the amount of artist input without their perspective.

Lori Lousararian-Hakola, Robert Norman and Paul Easton have been there for me throughout the years. They have listened to me and have answered my questions religiously. (These are three extraordinarily fair-minded people).

The Technical Department

This department consists of Ms. Gina Nardi of Nardi Art, LLC, Indianapolis, IN; Ms. Terri Balon-Bowden of Bal-Bow Grafix, Danville, IN; Ms. Susan Pearce of Susan Pearce Design, Yucca Valley, CA and Ms. Pam Schmid at Desert Copy, Yucca Valley, CA are to be applauded for their art creation and their assistance with original manuscript; Mr. Scott Souza aka Great Scott Souza, Hawaii Web Design Studio, Honolulu, HI, for help with QR code creation; Lanna Monday Emmett and Zane Sturgill at The Napoleon Hill Foundation, Wise, VA for their email and website assistance. I thank each one of you for your priceless patience and discerning skillset.

Audio Video Department

Some might ask, "Why would you have an audio/video department for a written book?" In this case it's all based on the Quick Response Codes (QR Codes). These codes are used for educational purposes throughout this book and would not have been possible without Zane Sturgill and Mr. Don M. Green of The Napoleon Hill Foundation, Wise, VA; Gary Chappell at Chappell Enterprises, Buffalo Cove, IL; Vic Conant, Chairman of the Board at Nightingale-Conant, Wheeling,

IL; "Video Bob" Stevenson of Pro Video, Yucca Valley, CA, and Dan and Hamik at AV Tape Transfer House, Hollywood, CA. What you see and what you hear would not be possible without the work, help and approval from the above. Thank you all!

Lifelong Mentor Department

Here, I would have to start at age twenty, with the first person to place a copy of *Think and Grow Rich* into my hands. My boss, Mr. Ed McCarthy at Inland Container Corporation, Indianapolis, IN. I'm almost certain Ed has no idea I still remember his name, and pretty sure he does not remember me. Unbeknownst to him, he set the blaze which led to my burning desire to eventually help others. This book led me back to the early 1900s to Andrew Carnegie and his inspiration given to Napoleon Hill. Thank you, Ed!

I have always been "over the top" with learning the knowledge and understanding the spirit of Zig Ziglar. I'm not sure how many of you have had these words spoken to you from Zig, as I have—"I love you too Randey," however, if you have, you know that feeling and how those words from such a man can carry through a lifetime. Thank you Zig!

I feel compelled to mention my newest mentor and person I wish to emulate, Mr. Don M. Green, CEO of The Napoleon Hill Foundation. Likewise, I have learned so much from Don in such a short amount of time, it's almost frightening. He always seems to give me the answer before I even ask the question. I could fill an entire book regarding Don and you never know, I just might!

Which brings me to my dear friend of fifty years, Mr. Clark H. Byrum of Key Life Insurance Co, Indianapolis, IN and the Clark H. Byrum School of Business, Marian University, Indianapolis, IN. Clark has given me so much prudent advice over the years, I cannot thank him enough.

Supply Department

I would like to thank the entire trustworthy crew, and especially John Schulman, at Ron's Automotive in Yucca Valley, CA, for their endless supply of writing pens in which every word of the *Think and Grow Through Art and Music* manuscript was written.

Faith and Confidence Department

Here, I salute three men who wake up and go to bed with the word "persistence" at the forefront of their minds!

First is the one and only Mr. Don M. Green, CEO of The Napoleon Hill Foundation, Wise, VA, whose name keeps popping up in these acknowledgments. There is a reason for that. If I ever had a hero based on noble deeds and qualities, it would surely be Hero Don M. Green. Not only did he have faith in me and my writing, he also contributed by writing the foreword, as well as two QR Code podcasts. The chapter 7 podcast is on Decision and the chapter 8 podcast is a subject that is second nature to him—Persistence. Don is a visionary, who follows through on what he says he will do. When he said, "We will get a publisher for *Think and Grow Through Art and Music*," I never doubted him or lost a minute's sleep. I knew if he said it, then it would be. Don is a blessing of unparalleled proportion, and I thank him for having faith in me. To sum up, I share these five words, as I simply and honestly say, "I love you, Don Green."

Secondly, a hearty applause goes to Mr. Dan Strutzel, President of Inspire Productions (Antioch, Illinois) and past V.P. of Nightingale-Conant Corp. As some musicians are considered musician's musicians, Dan could be considered a publisher's publisher. He is to be commended for his determination and persistence, as he prevailed in landing the most perfect publisher I could have ever hoped for in G&D Media, New York, NY.

Thirdly, I would also like to extend my sincere appreciation to Mr. Gilles Dana, President/CEO of G&D Media and his entire staff for having faith and seeing the potential in *Think and Grow Through Art and Music*. G&D Media is one of the most innovative, dependable and team-oriented publishers in the marketplace today. Thank you, G&D Media!

My heartfelt appreciation is allocated equally between Don Green, Dan Strutzel, and Gilles Dana, as these three extraordinary men all display an unsurpassed skill set.

The Editing Department

I would like to shine a light on Meghan Day Healey of G&D Media for her direction, meticulous organization and professional suggestions, and above all her pleasing personality. I could never have been blessed with a more perfect individual to professionally edit this book. This honor goes to Robert Johnson Jr. Unbeknownst to him, his assurance was monumental and gave me the vote of confidence that I needed at such a touch and go time in the infancy of *Think and Grow Through Art and Music*.

My first vote came from my mate for fate, my star on a cloudy night . . . my wife, Cindyrae. She was first to say, I think you've written a masterpiece and it will inspire anyone with a desire to succeed. You can read more about her later, as she heads up the "Love and Devotion Department."

My second vote came from Mr. Don M. Green. After realizing we have the opportunity to help thousands upon thousands who aspire to have a successful career in the field of music and art, Don said, "Let's send this over to Bob, our editor, for his opinion." In other words, Don said, "Let's move forward." I was tingling with appreciation on the inside when Don declared those words.

Six other most relevant and beneficial words I heard during that time, are still playing in my mind today. When I met The Napoleon

Hill Foundation's editor, Robert Johnson Jr., in person, he said these words, "This is very well written Randey." Those six words played over and over in my mind, the entire time Dan Strutzel at Inspired Production was securing a publisher. I not only thank Bob for editing *Think and Grow Through Art and Music* and suggesting a few changes and deletions, I also thank him for those six words in which I rode on for over a year. Words such as his can be so powerful, especially when coming from a man of such high esteem.

The Love and Devotion Department

Here is the fun part where I get to thank my number one fan, my cheering section, my editor-in-chief, my sweet loving "wife for life," Cindyrae Faulkner. This book would never have been finished in this style, without her dedication and assistance. Her constructive PMA, coupled with her cheerfulness to make changes upon changes, and hours upon hours of typing, reading, re-reading and editing, could only be exceeded by the eminent role she played in our Master Mind Alliance. There were many a morning I woke up at 5 a.m. to write and assemble, only to find she had been typing since 4 a.m. God could not have given me a more devoted partner in a Master Mind Alliance and for this I am extremely grateful. I optimistically dedicate my love and life to her well-being and happiness in the future and for all eternity. Thank You!

May God richly bless each and every soul I have mentioned above!

About the Author

While writing computer programs for a large corporation in 1969, Randey Faulkner was introduced to *Think and Grow Rich*. Within one year of devouring this book, he paid cash for a brand-new Jaguar XKE and a Nova Super Sport. One day while walking out to the cars, he became awestruck by the fact that he owned two new vehicles, whereas one year earlier, he had a car parked there that he could hardly afford to put tires on. To him, this seemed like magic. That is when he started his small business called "Do You Believe In Magic?" He made a flip chart with photos of these two cars, and for a short time became a motivational speaker explaining how he acquired them, by applying Napoleon Hill's principles in *Think and Grow Rich*. His closing line was, "If I can do it, so can you!" For the past 50 years he has been sharing these same principles, as well as *Think and Grow Rich*, with any and all.

He has applied Napoleon Hill's principles in every aspect of his life, including his Goodyear/Michelin Tire Businesses, Real Estate, and Music Productions.

After retiring in Hawaii, he decided to move back to Southern California so that he could fulfill his life's passion in completing an idea that came to him in the early 1980s. He started actual work on his project in the 1990s. His passion was to write a book to help anyone, especially younger folks, who aspire to become a professional in the field of art and music.

His desire was to emulate Napoleon Hill's method by performing research and interviews with those who have gained success in the art and music industry. He initially turned to Chet Atkins as a source of introductions to successful musicians and artists. When Chet slipped away from us in 2001, he turned to Mr. Les Paul for the same source of introductions. Here he spent four plus years, off and on, under Les' direction. From there he performed research and continued to interview successful artists and musicians to complete his life's dream of publishing *Think and Grow Through Art and Music*.

Notes

Notes

Notes